Frederick Robertson Jones

History of Taxation in Connecticut

1636-1776

Frederick Robertson Jones

History of Taxation in Connecticut
1636-1776

ISBN/EAN: 9783337339067

Printed in Europe, USA, Canada, Australia, Japan

Cover: Foto ©ninafisch / pixelio.de

More available books at **www.hansebooks.com**

JOHNS HOPKINS UNIVERSITY STUDIES

IN

HISTORICAL AND POLITICAL SCIENCE

˙ HERBERT B. ADAMS, Editor

History is past Politics and Politics are present History—*Freeman*

FOURTEENTH SERIES

III

COLONIAL ORIGINS

OF

NEW ENGLAND SENATES

By F. L. RILEY, A. M.

Fellow in History. J. H. U.

CONTENTS.

	PAGE.
INTRODUCTION	7

CHAPTER I.—MASSACHUSETTS.

Section I.—Governmental Beginnings	9
Section II.—The Executive Function	11
Section III.—The Judicial Function	16
Section IV.—The Legislative Function	18
Section V.—The Proposed Constitution of 1778	23
Section VI.—The Constitution of 1780	25

CHAPTER II.—CONNECTICUT.

Section I.—Governmental Beginnings	28
Section II.—The Executive Function	31
Section III.—The Judicial Function	33
Section IV.—The Legislative Function	36
Section V.—The Constitution of 1818	38

CHAPTER III.—NEW HAMPSHIRE.

Section I.—Governmental Beginnings	40
Section II.—The Executive Function	41
Section III.—The Judicial Function	43
Section IV.—The Legislative Function	46
Section V.—The Constitution of 1776	48
Section VI.—The Proposed Constitution of 1779	51
Section VII.—The Proposed Constitution of 1781	51
Section VIII.—The Constitution of 1783-4	52

CHAPTER IV.—RHODE ISLAND.

Section I.—Governmental Beginnings	54
Section II.—The Executive Function	59
Section III.—The Judicial Function	60
Section IV.—The Legislative Function	64
Section V.—The Constitution of 1842	66

5

CHAPTER V.—CONCLUSIONS.   PAGE.

Section I.—Origin of the New England Senates.......................... 69
Section II.—Forces Which Gave Direction to their Development.
    1. Limitation of the Number of Counsellors....................... 72
    2. Extent of Authority and Growth of the Colonies............. 72
    3. Illogical Principle upon which Power was Distributed...... 73
    4. Introduction of the Idea of a Complete Separtion of the
       Functions of Government....................................... 74
    5. Inter-Colonial Influences... 74
    6. English Charters and Precedents................................ 74
Section III.—Inherited Characteristics of the Senates.
    1. Size.. 76
    2. Personnel... 76
    3. Basis of Selection... 76
    4. Term of Office... 76

INTRODUCTION.

The American Senates, like all other great institutions, are not the products of invention but of growth ; a growth, too, which required more than a century to mature. They appear in our early State Constitutions as the results of a series of evolutions which are synchronous with our colonial history. This research is designed to trace ultimately[1] the successive steps of this development from its inception in colonial institutions to its final results as embodied in our State and Federal Constitutions. It is undertaken with the desire of determining, as far as practicable, the different forces which have given direction to this growth and the relative effect of native and foreign influences in the formation of the finished product. Since the greater part of this study is confined to a period antedating the separation of governmental functions, it necessitates a more or less comprehensive treatment of all the departments of colonial government. The Colonial Councils, from which the State Senates evolved, originally exercised a power which was three-fold,—executive, judicial and legislative. In the course of time, however, they lost their executive and judicial authority, as is shown in the following pages, and were thus merged into State Senates in the present sense of the word.

---

[1] The present study, however, is confined to the New England colonies, a continuation of the work being reserved for a future publication.

COLONIAL ORIGINS OF NEW ENGLAND SENATES.

CHAPTER I.

MASSACHUSETTS.

Section I.—Governmental Beginnings.

Historians and jurists of rare ability have subjected the first charter of the Massachusetts Bay Colony to the most searching analyses in order to determine the nature and extent of the power which it conferred upon the patentees. The conclusions which have been reached on this point are by no means harmonious. Some maintain that the charter conferred no powers apart from those exercised by ordinary trading corporations, and that it was therefore totally inadequate for the establishment of a commonwealth in a foreign land;[1] while others, no

---

[1] Lodge's *Short History of English Colonies in America*, 412; Oliver's *Puritan Commonwealth*, 52, 76; *Massachusetts Historical Soc. Proceedings*, 1869, 166–188. An excellent account of the limitations of this instrument is also given in Brooks Adams' *Emancipation of Mass.*, Ch. I. "Some of the best politicians and lawyers, after the Revolution, Somers, Holt, Treby and Ward noted the following defects in this charter: That being originally granted to a great company resident in England, it was wholly inapplicable to the circumstances of a distant colony, because it gave the body politic no more jurisdiction than every other corporation within the Kingdom; that no authority was conferred to call special assemblies, wherein should appear the delegates of the people, because representation was expressly excluded

9

less eminent, contend that the colonists in erecting a civil
government upon this basis neither violated the laws of
England nor transgressed the limits of their prerogatives as
defined in the charter.[1]   However this may be, the transfer
of the charter to the colony in 1630 affected the political status
of the Assistants, or Counsellors very materially, since in the
inevitable confusion arising out of this shifting of the seat of
government, they were able to exchange the vaguely defined
powers of the charter for a more substantial authority based
upon the political necessities of the colony.   Hence their power
developed with astonishing rapidity.[2]   From " directors of a

---

by the clause requiring the presence of the freemen in the General Courts;
that no permission was given to raise money either on the colonists or on
strangers trading thither, because the King could not give an authority
which he did not himself possess; that it did not enable the legislative
body to erect various judicatories, either of admiralty, or probate of wills,
or of chancery, because that required such a special grant as did not here
exist." (Neal's *History of New England*, ed. 1741, II, 105–6; Chalmer's
Political Annals, I, 141–142).

[1] Prof. Joel Parker, the successor of Judge Story in the Cambridge Law
School maintains the following theses which he supports by a series of
cogent arguments: (1) That "the charter was not intended to be an act
for the incorporation of a trading or merchants' company merely.   But it
was a grant which contemplated the settlement of a colony, with power in
the corporated company to govern that colony"; (2) "The charter authorized the establishment of the government of the colony within the limits of
the territory to be governed as was done by vote to transfer the charter and
government"; (3) "The charter gave ample power of legislation and of
government for the plantation or colony, including power to legislate on
religious subjects in the manner in which the grantees and their associates
claimed and exercised the legislative power"; (4) "The charter authorized
the creation and erection of courts of judicature to hear and determine
causes and to render final judgments and cause execution to be done without
any appeal to the courts of England." (*Mass. and Its Early History*, Lowell
Institute Lectures, 1869, 357–439).   For further arguments pro and con
on this subject see Ellis' *Puritan Age in Mass.*, Ch. VII; Adams' *Emancipation of Mass.*, Ch. I.

[2] Within a few months three important acts were passed which gave the
Assistants powers that transcended the limits defined by the charter. 1. At
the first General Court held at Boston in October, 1630, the freemen,

company," with a limited term of office as contemplated by
the charter,[1] they soon rose to the dignity of magistrates[2] with
practically a life-tenure of office. Another short step made
them virtual "rulers of a commonwealth" with all the departments of government under their control.[3]

Section II.—The Executive Function.

In the exercise of executive power, however, they acted
more in accordance with the provisions of the charter than

---

through the influence of the newly arrived Governor and Assistants (Hutchinson's *Hist. of Mass.*, I, 30), who had been chosen in England (*Ib.*, 20),
delegated to the Assistants the privilege of choosing from among themselves
"a Goūn[r] & Deputy Goūn[r], whoe wth the Assistants should haue the power
of makeing lawes & chuseing officers to execute the same;" and retained
for themselves only the power of choosing Assistants "when they are to
be chosen." (*Mass. Col. Rec.*, I, 79.) Of course the practical result of this
last clause was a life-tenure for the Assistants. (Hutchinson, I, 30; Palfrey's
Compendious Hist. of New Eng., I, 123; Winthrop's *Hist. of New Eng.*, I, 85;
Hubbard's *Hist. of New Eng.*, 147). 2. Six months later it was voted that
these extraordinary powers which had been granted the Assistants might
be exercised by five or even a less number (*Mass. Col. Rec.*, I, 84), though
the charter required at least six Assistants and either the Governor or
Deputy Governor to constitute a quorum (*Ib.*, 11). 3. Two months later
(May 18, 1631), it was enacted that for the future "it shalbe lawfull for
the Coūmons to ppounde any pson or psons whome they shall desire to be
chosen Assistants, & if it be doubtfull whith[r] it be the great[r] pte of the
comons or not, it shalbe putt to the poll. The like course to be holden
when they, the said coūmons, shall see cause for any defect or misbehav[r] to
remoue any one or more of y[e] Assist[ts]." (*Mass. Col. Rec.*, I, 87.) The
obscurely-worded sentence which seems to have been appended as "a rider"
at the end of an act that would have been otherwise very liberal, created a
precedent for a permanent tenure of the magistracy, "since it required the
invidious and difficult process of a vote for the confirmation or removal of
Assistants already in office" (Palfrey, I, 123; Winthrop, I, 85). Hence
"the dignities, the emoluments and for a considerable time, the powers of
the government were monopolized by ten or twelve persons." (*Puritan
Com.*, 55; Hutchinson, I, 293, note).

[1] *Mass. Col. Rec.*, I, 10, 12.
[2] Grahame's *Col. Hist. of U. S.*, I, 162; *Puritan Com.*, 55, 56.
[3] See Prof. G. H. Haynes' *Representation and Suffrage in Mass.*, 1620–1691,
J. H. U. Studies, Twelfth Series, VIII–IX, Ch. 2.

when assuming the other functions of government. It is probably due to this cause that they were enabled to keep strictly intact, throughout the colonial period, this alone of all their original powers.

The first charter vested the executive function in the Governor, Deputy Governor and eighteen [1] Assistants or Counsellors.[2] Their general duties pertained to the transactions of "matters in the absence of the General Court."[3] Further details as to time and place of meeting, as well as the specific nature and scope of their duties, were to be determined as the exigencies of the colony might demand. Randolph, writing about 1676, says that the Council met in its executive capacity twice every week, and as often besides as it was convened by the Governor.[4]

---

[1] This number was not chosen, however, at any one time in the first fifty years after the transfer of the charter to the colony in 1630. (Palfrey, II, 233). During the earlier years from six to nine were generally chosen, vacancies being left for men of note who might come over. (Palfrey, I, 149; Hutchinson, I, 44-5). In 1658 the number was limited by law to fourteen. (*Mass. Col. Rec.*, IV, 1 pt. 1, 347). This law was repealed in 1641, yet the practice remained the same. (*Ib.*, 347; pt. 2, 32; 468, Palfrey, II, 28). On the next year Charles II demanded that not more than eighteen nor less than ten Assistants be chosen annually. (*Mass. Col. Rec.*, IV, pt. 2, 32; Perry's *Hist. Papers of the Amer. Col. Church*, 35). A special election was held in October 16, 1678, to bring the number up to eighteen in compliance with a demand of the home government. (*Mass. Col. Rec.*, V, 195). July 24, 1679, the King demanded "that the ancient number of Assistants be henceforth observed as by charter." (Hutchinson, I, 293; Chalmers, I, 451). This was observed until 1686 (*Mass. Col. Rec.*, V, 513), when the government passed into the control of a President and Council appointed by the Crown. (*Conn. Col. Rec.*, III, 207, note).

[2] Savage (Winthrop, II, 207, note) observes that without the Assistants "the Governor would have been nothing and with them his power seems to have been hardly more than that of *primus inter pares.*" He presided over the sittings of the Council and was entitled to one vote at all times, and two when there was a tie. (*Ibid;* Hutchinson, II, 15; Palfrey, III, 71-2, 74; Barry's *Hist. of Mass.*, II, 16, 17).

[3] *Mass. Col. Rec.*, I, 10; Chalmers, 137, 436.

[4] Randolph's *Present State of New England,* published in Perry's *Historical Papers of the American Colonial Church,* 2-3; Washburn's *Judicial History of Massachusetts,* 23.

Yet the exercise of this authority, as broadly outlined in the charter,[1] did not go unchallenged. Before the details of the Council's power could become crystallized into precedents which could be cited as historical grounds for its activity, it encountered the opposition of the Deputies. The latter attempted first to gain admittance to the executive Council, but failing in this, they tried to make it strictly dependent upon the General Court.[2] This acrimonious contest was finally settled by referring the matter to the elders—the sacred oracles of the colony—who, as usual, declared in favor of the patricians. Hence the composition and powers of the Executive Council remained *in statu quo.* The Deputies, frustrated in their first attempt to share the executive function with the Council, then resorted to various schemes, by which they still hoped to diminish its powers.[3]

---

[1] Chalmers' *Political Annals*, 137 ; *Mass. Col. Rec.*, I, 10.

[2] The first conflict arose in 1643, when the General Court committed the affairs of the colony during its recess to the Magistrates and the Deputies of Boston, Charlestown, Cambridge, Roxbury and Dorchester. (*Mass. Col. Rec.*, II, 46). This addition of Deputies to the Executive Council was opposed by the Magistrates, who contended that it was an infringement upon their charter rights. The controversy was renewed the next year when the Deputies made a proposition that the General Court issue commissions "whereby power was given to seven Magistrates and three Deputies and Mr. Ward (some time pastor of Ipswich and still a preacher) to order all affairs of the commonwealth in the vacancy" of that body. (Winthrop, II, 204-5). They contended in support of this act that "the Magistrates had no power out of the General Court but what must be derived" from it. This proposition was also rejected by the Assistants as "an innovation upon the charter." They were then tendered "a commission for war only," which they likewise rejected. They also refused to suspend the exercise of their executive power until the matter could be settled at the next General Court. (*Ibid.*, 204-206).

[3] Winthrop, II, 282-284. They enacted such "a body of law, with prescript penalties in all cases" that "nothing might be left to the discretion of the Magistrates." Many of them were agreed upon by the Magistrates, but they finally returned some with their non-concurrence. The Deputies then complained that the Magistrates "would have no laws." They also expressed opinions contrary to the decision of the Magistrates when acting in this capacity,—all of which tended "to weaken the authority of the Magistrates and their reputation with the people." (*Ibid.*).

In the second charter[1] provision was made for the establishment of a Council of twenty-eight members[2] to be chosen by the Assembly, subject to the approval of the Governor. The executive powers of this body differed somewhat from those which it had previously exercised. It was deprived of the power to grant land,[3] but in connection with the Governor, was given authority to nominate and appoint judges, commissioners of Oyer and Terminer, sheriffs, provosts, marshalls, justices of the peace and other officers of the "Council and Courts of Justice,"[4] to issue warrants for disposing of public revenues;[5] and to exercise martial law upon the inhabitants.[6] It also gave the entire executive authority into the hands of the Council upon the death or absence of the Governor and the Lieutenant Governor.[7] In addition to these duties, numerous other executive powers were granted it by the legislature from time to time.[8]

---

[1] The temporary and reactionary periods of Andros' rule demands no attention in this connection.

[2] This requirement was not always strictly observed. Between 1741 and 1766, whenever the Governor rejected any of the twenty-eight names suggested by the Assembly, their places were left vacant, the Assembly refusing to nominate others by way of retaliation. (Hutchinson, III, p. 152). This finally led to the formation of a list of "Mandamus Counsellors." (Palfrey, IV, 433).

[3] *Acts and Res. of the Prov. of Mass. Bay*, I, 17.

[4] *Ibid.*, 12; Douglass' *Summary of Amer.*, I, 473, 486.

[5] *Acts and Res.*, 16, 218; Randolph's *Pres. State of New England* in Perry, 19; Palfrey, III, 74.

[6] *Acts and Res.*, I, 18.

[7] *Ibid.*, 19, VII, 283, note; Poore's *Charters and Constitutions*, I, 953. The administration devolved upon the Council for the first time, July 7, 1701, though there was at that time some doubt as to whether the Council or its President should exercise this function. (Hutchinson, II, 117). In 1704, the Queen directed that under such circumstances the eldest counsellor should preside, but it was never observed, because contrary to the charter. (*Ibid.*, 191).

[8] They were given privileges to grant licenses for erecting buildings in Boston (*Acts and Res.*, I, 42, 405), admitting and removing settlers (*Ibid.*, 90, 194, 402); allowed to award bounties (*Ibid.*, 473), appoint commissioners

A conflict arose over the extent of power conferred by the clause which gave the Governor and Council authority to sign warrants for the disposal of public money. This struggle extended over a period of several years,[1] and was not ultimately settled until the formation of the constitution of 1780.[2]

(*Ibid.*, 385, 211, 473), reward services (*Ibid.*, 424), appoint certain courts (*Ibid.*, 719), reprieve condemned persons (Randolph's *Pres. State of New Eng.*), etc.

[1] This power seems to have been the first under the new charter to be assailed by the Representatives. In 1695 the legislature passed an act to the effect that "no public money be or ought to be disposed of by his excellency, the Governor, and Council, but for the uses and intents of, and according to the acts by which the said money is raised." (*Acts*, 170). This act was repealed by the King in Council a year later. (*Ibid.*, note). By degrees, however, the House "acquired from the Governor and Council the keys of the treasury," and by the year 1723, "no moneys could be issued without the vote of the House for that purpose" (Hutchinson, II, 266), and the right of the Representatives to originate money bills was undisputed. "But they went further and intrenched upon the charter rights of the Council and allowed no payment to be made for services until they had judged whether they were performed and had passed a special order for such payment." (*Ibid.*). They even voted that there should be paid out of the treasury to the Speaker of the House 300 pounds sterling "to be applied *as they should direct.*" After about three weeks of altercation, it was agreed that 100 pounds should be so allowed, and that 200 pounds be paid to such agent as should be chosen by the whole Court. (*Ibid.*, 272-3). The House gained the point at issue, and continued to designate the objects for which moneys were raised, thus leaving nothing to the discretion of the Governor and Council, until 1729, when Governor Shute vetoed an appropriation bill for this reason. (*Ibid.*, 322). The dispute which followed was settled unfavorably for the House. (*Ibid.*, 338-9). In 1732, the Representatives succeeded in passing a bill not materially differing from the old method. (*Ibid.*, 339). In 1733, they successfully claimed a right to audit the public accounts. In later years grants for the defense of the province were so made that the Governor and Council were restrained from drawing money from the treasury "for any other purpose." Governor Pownall submitted to this invasion only under protest, on January 25, 1758, though his predecessor had allowed it without complaint. (*Ibid.*, III, 66-67). In 1762, the House remonstrated against the method in which this power had been exercised, stating that it was taking away "their most darling privilege," and that it was "annihilating one branch of the Legislature." (*Ibid.*, 97). On this subject, see also Minot's *Hist. of Mass.*, II, 65 *et seq.*

[2] See *infra.*

Section III.—The Judicial Function.

One of the many serious defects of the first charter was its failure to provide for the erection of a judicial system. Upon the transference of the government to the colony, the Assistants took advantage of this defect and, realizing the necessities of the colony, clothed themselves in judicial ermine and transformed their court into a tribunal of justice.[1] Their magisterial power, once conceded[2] in time of necessity, remained very extensive during the existence of the first charter.[3] In this capacity they served not only in the General Court, which by the law of 1634, was declared "the chief civil power of the Commonwealth,"[4] but in the "great Quarter Court" of appeals established in 1635–6,[5] the semi-annual "Court of Assistants" organized in 1639,[6] as well as in the capacity of

---

[1] *Puritan Commonwealth*, 78.

[2] *Mass. Col. Rec.*, I, 89.

[3] Washburn's *Judicial Hist. of Mass.*, 42.

[4] *Col. Laws* (ed. 1660), 88. Latchford, in his *Plain Dealing*, written about 1640, says of the General Courts, "They have the power of Parliament, King's Bench, Common Pleas, Chancery, High Commission and Star Chamber, and all other Courts of England."

[5] *Mass. Col. Rec.*, I, 169; Hubbard, 243.

[6] *Col. Laws*, 23, 90. Randolph, writing in 1676, says: "There be two Courts of Assistants yearly kept at Boston by the Governor or Deputy Governor and the rest of the Magistrates upon the first Tuesday in March and the first Tuesday in September, to hear and determine all actions of appeal from inferior courts and all capital and criminal causes extending to life, member or banishment." (*Pres. State of New Eng.* in Perry's Historical Papers, etc., 3). They also exercised "admiralty jurisdiction and appellate jurisdiction in matters of probate." (Washburn, 30; Chalmers, 436). In fact, the jurisdiction of this Court was as extensive as that of the General Court (Washburn, 29) which retained only appellate power (*Col. Laws*, 45) except in chancery cases over which it exercised original jurisdiction until 1685, when a subordinate system of chancery was established. (Washburn, 28). After 1642 the General Court exercised appellate jurisdiction over criminal cases only. (*Col. Laws*, 199).

ex officio justices in the lower courts of the colony,[1] and individual magistrates in the town where they resided.[2]

Under the second charter, which left to the legislature the establishment of courts of judicature, the judicial power of the Governor and Council was greatly diminished.[3] In fact, they were granted jurisdiction only in cases of probate [4] and divorce. These duties, however, soon proved too onerous, and the Governor and Council, by the right of substitution which they possessed as a civil law court, created Judges of Probate in every county, from whose decisions appeals could be taken to them as a Supreme Court of Probate.[5] Thus, by the end of the colonial period, the Council had reduced its judicial duties to a minimum, retaining little more than appellate jurisdiction over a very limited field of judicature.

---

[1] Hutchinson, II, 21; *Mass. Col. Rec.*, I, 169, 175; Hubbard, 234.

[2] This seems to have been the origin of the civil jurisdiction of Justices of the Peace in Massachusetts, though Stearns (*Real Actions*, 506) thinks it began with the act of 1644, and Judge Parsons (*M. R.*, IV, 515) says that Justices of the Peace were not known as officers under the first charter. The limiting of their individual jurisdiction was first placed at 20 shillings, but was subsequently (1644) raised to 40. Randolph (*Pres. State of New Eng.* in Perry's Hist. Papers, 3) says that "every Magistrate is a Justice of the Peace and can determine any cause under forty shillings, can commit to prison and punish offenders for breach of laws and impose fines according to discretion." See Washburn, 36; also Chalmers, 37; *Mass. Col. Rec.*, I, 276.

[3] The powers of the General and the Assistants' Courts were granted to a Superior Court, those of the County Courts to Courts of Common Pleas and Quarter Sessions, while the regular Probate Courts exercised a part of the former powers of the County Courts and the jurisdiction of the Magistrates and Commissioners of small causes was exercised by Justices of the Peace. Probate and divorce matters were left to the Governor and Council, whose decisions were rendered by a major vote of the whole Court. (Hutchinson, II, 451-2).

[4] Washburn, 138, 187.

[5] Washburn, 187. When the Legislature undertook to exercise the power of creating similar courts, the King negatived the act.

Section IV.—The Legislative Function.

The legislative power of the Assistants, which, after the transfer of the first charter to the colony,[1] rose so quickly to high-tide, soon began to ebb with even greater rapidity. Only a short time after the reaction set in, this oligarchy[2]—for such the government under the Board of Assistants had become— was stripped of its power and replaced by a representative government, which became permanently established in 1634.[3]

---

[1] See *supra.*   [2] Chalmers, I, 157–8.

[3] Opposition to the Assistants originated over a question of taxation. On February 3, 1632–3, they levied a tax of eight pounds upon the inhabitants of Watertown (*Mass. Col. Rec.*, I, 93), which evoked from these people a protest that "it was not safe to pay moneys after that sort, for fear of bringing themselves and posterity into bondage." (Winthrop, I, 84; Lodge, 345). Although this particular case seems to have been amicably settled, the freemen of the colony were aroused to an assertion of their rights, and a number of reforms followed in its wake. Two months later (April 3, 1633) the powers of the Governor were definitely defined (Winthrop, I, 86), and in another month (May 9, 1633) the powers of the Assistants were restricted by a sweeping act of reform which required: 1, That the Governor, Deputy Governor and Assistants should be elected by the freemen; 2, That these officers should be "new chosen every year"; and 3, That there should be "two of every plantation appointed to confer" with the Governor and Assistants "about raising of a public stock." (*Mass. Col. Rec.*, I, 95; Winthrop, I, 90, 91; Hutchinson, I, 30; Holmes' *Annals of America*, I, 258). The last of these acts meant that the Court of Assistants was no longer recognized as a representative assembly, and that the people were determined to levy taxes only through their representatives.

The rapid acquisition of authority by representatives of the towns, and the corresponding loss of power by the Assistants, is remarkable. In 1632, representatives of the towns were permitted only to "advise" and "agree" with the Assistants on matters of taxation. Two years later they were instructed "to meet and consider of such matters as they were to take in order" at the next General Court. (Winthrop, I, 152 *et seq.*). But when they met this time they questioned the right of the Assistants to make laws, and contended that the charter granted such privileges only to the General Court. In spite of the Governor's attempt to evade the issue (*Ibid.*, 153) a body of twenty-four representatives appeared at the next General Court, and were fully incorporated into the legislative body of the colony. At

At this date the General Court became the legislature of the colony, and was composed of the Assistants who represented the colony as a whole and the Deputies who represented the towns.

For the next ten years both bodies sat as one house and usually voted together, " without any distinction, the major part of the whole number determining the vote." The number of Assistants, however, was limited by the charter, while the Deputies were allowed to increase with the formation of new towns. Hence there arose a struggle for existence, on the part of the Assistants. A Council for life was established in order to strengthen their ranks.[1] Yet had not the Assistants taken the following precaution, they would have lost "all their

---

this Court several radical reforms were introduced. Besides electing a new man for Governor, and fining the Assistants for their past conduct, the freemen enacted: 1, That the General Court alone had power to admit freemen ; 2, To make laws, to elect and remove officers, and to define their duties ; 3, To raise moneys and taxes and to dispose of lands; 4, That there were to be no trials for life or banishment except by a jury, or by the General Court; 5, That there were to be four General Courts held annually which were not to be dissolved without their consent ; and 6, That Deputies were to be elected and given "the full power & voyces of all the . . . ffreemen, deryved to them for the makeing & establishing of lawes, graunting of lands, &c., & to deale in all other affaires of the comonwealth wherein the ffreemen haue to doe, the matter of eleccon of magistrates & other officers onely excepted, wherein euy freeman is to gyve his owne voyce." (*Mass. Col. Rec.*, I, 117-9; Hutchinson, I, 39-40; Grahame, I, 169).

[1] At a General Court held March 3, 1635-6, it was ordered that at the next election there should be chosen "a certaine number of Magistrates for tearme of their lives." (*Mass. Col. Rec.*, I, 167). This act so contrary to both the spirit and the letter of the Charter (*Ibid.*, 10), was passed through the combined influence of the Assistants and the clergy (Oliver's *Puritan Commonwealth*, 63), ostensibly to conform to the teachings of the Bible, but really to counteract the rapidly developing power of the freemen, by tempting over to the colony "some of the peers and other leading men who might expect at home, in due season, to be raised to the upper house." (Winthrop, I, 219-220, note). It was virtually repealed on June 6, 1639. (*Ibid.*, 363-4; Hubbard, 244; *Mass. Col. Rec.*, I, 167, 264). Savage (Winthrop, I, 364, note) observes that this is probably the only instance of an election for life to any legislative or executive office in our country.

weight in the legislative part of the government."[1] Through
their influence, it was enacted in 1635 that " noe lawe, order, or
sentence shall passe as an act of the Court, without the consent
of the great^r pte of the magistrates on the one pte, & the
great^r number of the deputyes on the other pte; & for want
of such accorde, the cause or order shalbe suspended, &
if either ptie think it soe materiall, there shalbe forthwith
a comitté chosen, the one halfe by the magistrates, & the
other halfe by the deputyes, & the comittee soe chosen to
elect an vmpire, who togeather shall have power to heare &
determine the cause in question."[2] This act, however, seems
to have been soon forgotten in the conflicts[3] which arose over
the exercise of the " negative power." The Assistants maintained that they had a charter right to such a power, while
the Deputies, being in the majority, contended for a joint vote
on all matters. These struggles finally resulted in the intro-

---

[1] Hutchinson, I, 396–7.   [2] *Mass. Col. Rec.*, I, 170.

[3] The first occasion for such a disagreement arose over the request of Mr.
Hooker and his congregation for permission to remove to Connecticut. The
Governor, two Assistants and fifteen Deputies favored the request, while the
Deputy Governor, five Assistants and ten Deputies opposed it. Thus the
majority vote of the two bodies taken separately differed, but on a joint
ballot it stood eighteen to sixteen against the Assistants. The Assistants,
however, maintained their right to negative the vote of the Deputies, and
were successful through the influence of Mr. Cotton, who preached a sermon
on this subject at an interval given for fasting and prayer, when the struggle
had reached its height. The Deputies yielded only in this particular case,
without a final concession of the point. (Winthrop, I, 167–9; Hutchinson,
I, 47). For the prevention of such dead-locks in the future, the act cited
above was then passed. These struggles finally terminated in the celebrated
case concerning the possession of a hog. On this point a majority of the
two bodies disagreed upon a separate vote. The Deputies insisted upon a
joint ballot, which gave them a majority. Though the "sow business" was
never decided, the controversy resulted in the settlement of the constitutional question in dispute. (Winthrop, II, 83–86, 139–143). The Magistrates offered the next year to surrender their negative power if the freemen
would consent that their representatives should not exceed them in number
and should be " elected by the shires instead of the towns." The proposition
was rejected and probably never again renewed. (Winthrop, II, 214).

duction of the bicameral system, and in granting to each body
a negative over all the legislative acts of the other.[1]

From the date of this separation, March, 25, 1644, the two
bodies were distinct, and their powers began to differentiate.
The Deputies became what Chalmers calls "the democratic
branch of the legislature,"[2] while the Council took on the
functions of an upper house, though still retaining its separate
position as an executive advisory body.

In its subsequent evolution, as a branch of the legislature,
the Council underwent one radical change in membership.
This was the removal of its two *ex officio* members,—the
Governor and the Lieutenant Governor. The former ceased
to be a member of the Legislative Council in 1716[3] and the

---

[1] See Prof. T. F. Moran's *Rise and Development of the Bicameral System in
America*, J. H. U. Studies, Thirteenth Series, V, 8–13. This order, not by
hurtfully withdrawing a power from the Magistrates as had been attempted,
but by beneficially conferring an equal power upon the Deputies, determined the great contention about the negative voice and completed the
frame of the internal government of Massachusetts, destined to undergo no
further change for forty years." (Palfrey, I, 259). A modification of this
law was soon found necessary in judicial matters, since it would have pre-
vented any decision in many cases. It was, therefore, agreed in 1652, that
the veto power should be exercised only in legislative matters and that the
two houses should vote together in their judicial capacity, when they were
unable to reach a conclusion separately. (*Mass. Col. Rec.*, III, 179; IV, pt.
1, 82; Hutchinson, I, 134–5).

[2] *Polit. Annals*, 166. Douglass (*Summary*, I, 213–4) calls the Councils the
"aristocratical" and the Representatives the "democratic" elements of the
colonial legislatures.

[3] Under the first charter, the Council was composed of the Assistants, the
Governor and the Deputy Governor. It was presided over by the Governor
or, in his absence, by the Deputy Governor, who was not given a veto power
and was therefore in 1641 allowed a vote in its proceedings. His power as
a presiding officer was little more than that of the other members. If he
refused to put to vote a question opposed to his views, it could be done by
any other member of the body. (Hutchinson, I, 62–3). The second charter
gave him a veto power, but was silent as to whether he should be considered
a member of the Council in its legislative capacity. Since departures from
old precedents were made only by degrees, his claims to a seat were asserted
and conceded only at intervals. Lord Bellomont (1699–1700) and Governor

latter in 1767,[1] but both continued to hold their positions in this body when it acted in an executive capacity.

There was also an important change in the relations between the two branches of the Legislature. The Council lost the power to originate money bills, and this function came to be exercised by the Deputies alone. On this point Hutchinson observes that the House had " by degrees acquired from the Governor and Council the keys of the treasury and no money could be issued without the vote of the House for that pur-

---

Dudley (1702–1716) considered themselves not only members, but heads of the Council in both its executive and legislative capacities. They sat with the Counsellors, directed their debates and proposed all their business. The Governors who came into office after 1716 neglected to contend for such privileges and thus ceased to be regarded as members of the legislative Council.

[1] It was evidently intended for the Lieutenant Governor to be an *ex officio* member of the upper house of the legislature under the second charter as he had been under the first. Mr. Stoughton, the first Lieutenant Governor under the second charter, though not at first elected a member of the Council was considered " a Counsellor, *ex officio*, and voted and was upon committees the whole year." (*Acts and Resolves of Prov. of Mass. Bay*, VII, 5, note; Hutchinson, II, 174). At the second election he was regularly chosen one of the twenty-eight Counsellors as well as Lieutenant Governor, and was therefore doubly entitled to a seat in that body. His immediate successors also attended the meetings of the Council whether so selected or not, but they voted in its proceedings only when elected as Counsellors. In 1732 the rights of the Lieutenant Governor to an *ex efficio* seat in the Council when sitting in its legislative capacity was first challenged in the case of Mr. Phipps, who having been elected Lieutenant Governor against the desire of the Governor, was forbidden by the Governor to sit in that body " unless he should be elected by the Assembly and approved by the Governor." The question was finally settled in 1767 when Lieutenant-Governor Hutchinson failed to be elected to the Council. He was in constant attendance upon the meetings of the Council during the first session after his defeat, but "did not vote nor take any share in the debates." At the second session, however, his attendance was characterized by the House as "a new and additional instance of ambition and lust of power" (Hutchinson, III, 175 *et seq.*), and in spite of the efforts of the Governor and other friends, the House successfully maintained its position and the Lieutenant-Governor ceased to be an *ex officio* member of the upper branch of the Legislature. (*Ibid.*, 176–7).

pose."[1]   Hence, in 1744 the Governor requested the Assembly
to grant him and his Council power " to draw upon the treasurer " as occasion might require.[2]

Section V.—The Proposed Constitution of 1778.

During the revolutionary period the Council retained the
powers which had been granted by the second charter.[3]   But
the necessity for a more perfect constitution was soon recognized by the people, and efforts were early made to prepare
one, although the perturbed state of society, occasioned by
the war was not very favorable to such an undertaking.[4]   To
meet this necessity a committee appointed by the General

---

[1] *Hist. of Mass.*, II, 266, 303 ; III, 66.   The struggles over the exercise of
this power by the House and its effect upon the executive authority of the
Council has been noted in detail.   See *supra*, p. 15, note 1.

[2] Douglass' *Summary*, I, 473.   In the preceding treatment, the development of the Council in the Plymouth colony has been omitted because
the affairs of that settlement exerted little or no influence upon the
constitutional development of Massachusetts into which it was merged in
1691.   See Moore's *Lives of the Governors of New Plymouth and Mass. Bay,*
228.   The history of the Council of New Plymouth is, nevertheless, unique
because of the peculiar way in which it originated.   Upon the death of
Governor Carver in 1621, William Bradford was chosen Governor and he
"being not yet recovered of his ilnes, in which he had been near y⁰ point
of death Isaak Allerton was chosen to be an Assistante unto him." (Bradford's *Hist. of Plymouth Plantation* in Mass. Hist. Coll., Fourth Series, Vol.
III, 101).   This choice of an Assistant which was made, not as a matter of
principle but as a temporary expedient, furnished the precedent for a permanent change in the constitution of the colony. · The number of Assistants
was afterwards increased to five (1624) and then to seven (1633).   Their
duties were at first confined to the executive and judicial departments, but
with the introduction of representative government they became a part of
the law-making body of the colony.   See Prof. G. H. Haynes' *Representation
and Suffrage in Mass.*, 1620–1691, J. H. U. Studies, Twelfth Series, VIII–
IX, Chapter V.

[3] Bradford's *Hist. of Mass.*, 40 *et seq.*

[4] *Ibid.*, 42.

Assembly reported to that body a draft of a constitution in January, 1778, which was rejected by the people.[1]

In this constitution the Senate is a more or less accurate reproduction of the Council of the second charter. Article XXXII required that all laws which "refer to and mention the Council" should be "construed to extend to the Senate."[2] Both instruments provided for the annual election of twenty-eight members of this body[3]—by the Assembly, according to the charter, but by the freemen according to the constitution.[4] Both required a residence qualification,[5] but the constitution added to this a property[6] and a religious[7] qualification, and disqualified certain other officers of the State from a seat in either branch of the General Court.[8] The authority of the Council under this constitution, as under the charter, was principally executive and legislative,—its judicial power being restricted to the trial of impeachments.[9]

When sitting in a legislative capacity both the Senate and the House of Representatives had equal rights "to originate or reject any bill, resolve or order or to propose amendments; except in case of money bills, which were to originate in the House of Representatives only.[10]

The Governor and Senate were to constitute the executive body of the State, the former still retaining his position as *primus inter pares*.[11] The executive power of the Governor, exclusive of the Upper House, was still very limited. With the advice and consent of the Senate, however, he could march

---

[1] *Ibid.*, 140. This was done chiefly because it contained no Bill of Rights. Still it is important in this connection, since it embodies the political ideas of a representative body of the people at that time, and serves as a connecting link between the colonial and state governments.

[2] A draft of this constitution is given in Appendix to Bradford's *Hist. of Mass.*

[3] Constitution, Art. VIII.

[4] *Ibid.*, Art. IX.   [5] *Ibid.*, Art. III.   [6] *Ibid.*, Art. III.

[7] *Ibid.*, Art. XXIX.   [8] *Ibid.*, Art. IV.   [9] *Ibid.*, Art. XX.

[10] *Ibid.*, Art. XIV.   [11] *Ibid.*, Art. XVII, XXII.

the militia out of the State;[1] prorogue the General Court;[2] lay an embargo and prohibit the exportation of any commodity for a limited time;[3] appoint all officers, both civil and military, whose appointment was not reserved to the General Court,[4] and sign warrants for the disposal of all public money, "agreeably to the acts and resolves of the General Court."[5] "In case of a vacancy in the office of Governor and Lieutenant Governor," the executive authority was to devolve upon "the major part of the Senate."[6]

Section VI.—*The Constitution of* 1780.

A second and more successful effort at constitution-making was made in 1780.[7] This instrument marks the last step in the evolution of the Senate. Then for the first time in the history of Massachusetts, were the executive, legislative and judicial powers emphatically declared "separate and distinct."[8] The powers formerly exercised by the Council were, therefore, delegated to two separate bodies,[9]—a Senate, which performed the legislative, and a newly created Council, which performed the executive and advisory function. The qualifications for

---

[1] *Ibid.*, Art. XVII.   [2] *Ibid.*

[3] *Ibid.*, Art. XXI.   [4] *Ibid.*, Art. XIX.

[5] *Ibid.*, Art. XXXII. This limit to the power of the Council had been a cause of contention for several years. See *supra.*

[6] *Ibid.*, Art. XVIII.

[7] A copy of this constitution is given in Poore's *Charters and Constitutions,* I, 956–973.

[8] Bill of Rights, Art. XXX. Yet "all causes of marriage, divorce and alimony and appeals from the judges of probate" were to be "heard and determined by the Governor and Council" until the General Court should make other provisions. (Chap. III, Art. 5). These were the last remnants of judicial power exercised by the Governor and Council under the second charter.

[9] The seats of senators elected to the Council were declared vacant. (Chap. II, Sec. 3, Art. II).

membership in each body were the same,[1] and their members
were chosen at the same time and in the same way—a fact
which suggests their common origin.[2] This method of election
was of a double nature and combined the practices under both
charters—an election by the people and then by the General
Court.[3]

The Executive Council consisted of nine persons besides
the Lieutenant Governor,[4] five of whom constituted a quorum.
It was convened at the discretion of the Governor, "for the
ordering and directing the affairs of the commonwealth according to the laws of the land."[5] As under the second charter,
the Council assumed the functions of the chief executive upon
the vacancy of the office of Governor and Lieutenant Governor.[6] With the advice and consent of the Council, the
Governor could exercise the pardoning power,[7] appoint judicial
officers, fill vacancies under certain conditions,[8] and appoint
such officers of the continental army as were allowed to the
State by the Confederation of the United States. The power
to advise the Governor as to the signing of warrants for the
disposition of public moneys, which was first granted to the

---

[1] These qualifications were "a freehold within the commonwealth of the
value of three hundred pounds," "personal estate to the value of six hundred
pounds," a residence of five years within the State and a residence within
the district for which he is chosen at the time of his election. (Chap. II,
Sec. 2, Art. V).

[2] Members of both bodies were elected by the Senators and Representatives on a joint ballot from a list of forty names which were chosen by the
people "to be Counsellors and Senators." (Chap. I, Sec. 2, Art. I; Chap.
II, Sec. 3, Art. II).

[3] Chap. I, Sec. 2, Articles I, II.

[4] Under the charters the Governor and Lieutenant Governor came to be
members of the Council only in its executive capacity. See *supra.*

[5] Chap. II, Sec. I, Art. IV; *Ibid.*, Sec. 3, Art. I.

[6] Chap. II, Sec. 3, Art. VI.

[7] Chap. II, Sec. 1, Art. VIII. Under the second charter the Governor
and Council were allowed to grant only reprieves, while the power to grant
pardons rested with the General Court.

[8] *Ibid.*, Art. IX.

Council by the second charter, was renewed in the Constitution of 1780 with a few exceptions.[1]

The legislative department was composed of a Senate[2] and a House of Representatives, each of which had a negative on the other.[3] The two bodies differed as to privileges in only two respects: (1), The Senate had power to try impeachments,[4] and (2), The House had exclusive right to originate money bills.[5]

---

[1] *Ibid.*, Art. XI. These exceptions applied to "such sums as may be appropriated for the redemption of bills of credit or treasurer's notes or for the payment of interest."

[2] This body consisted of thirty-one members,—nine out of the list of forty returned for "Counsellors and Senators" (*supra*, 26, note 2) being chosen for the former office. The Senators were apportioned according to districts (Chap. I, Sec. 2, Art. I).

[3] Chap. I, Sec. 1, Art. I. This question was brought up and settled under the first charter. See *supra.*

[4] Chap. I, Sec. 2, Art. VIII. The party so convicted was, nevertheless, "liable to indictment, trial, judgment and punishment according to the laws of the land."

[5] Chap. I, Sec. 3, Art. VII. This power was acquired under the second charter. See *supra.*

CHAPTER II.

CONNECTICUT.

Section I.—Governmental Beginnings.

Whatever may have been the occasion for the removal of the inhabitants of Newtown (Hartford), Dorchester (Windsor) and Watertown (Wethersfield) from their first location in Massachusetts to the region of the Connecticut River,[1] they carried with them the form, if not the spirit, of the political and religious institutions of the mother colony,[2] under whose government they continued for several months after their removal.[3] Their only assembly was a court held at each town in turn and composed of two magistrates from each, except when

---

[1] Doyle (*Eng. Colonies in Amer.*, II, 159) thinks that they did not withdraw "out of any dissatisfaction or with any craving for political changes," while Johnston (*Conn., Amer. Commonwealth Series*, 64) characterizes this removal as "a secession of the democratic element from Massachusetts." On this subject see also Trumbull's *Memorial History of Hartford County*, I, 19 *et seq.*

[2] Morey's *Genesis of a Written Constitution*, Annals of Amer. Acad., I, 551; Johnston's *Genesis of a New Eng. State*, J. H. U. Studies, First Series, 13–14; Palfrey, I, 233; Bond's *Hist. of Watertown, Mass.*, I, 980; Hartley's *Hartford in the Olden Time*, 49; Stiles' *Hist. of Ancient Windsor*, 25, note; Loomis and Calhoun's *Judic. and Civil Hist. of Conn.*, 2. Even their Massachusetts magistrates and ministers (except the minister at Watertown) removed with them. On the extent of authority delegated to these Massachusetts magistrates see Hazard, I, 322.

[3] Andrews' *River Towns of Conn.*, J. H. U. Studies, Seventh Series, VII, VIII, IX, 78–81; Loomis and Calhoun, 3–4; *Memorial Hist. of Hartford County*, I, 105.

Pynchon, the Magistrate from Agawam[1] (Springfield) was present and raised the number to seven. Its members were commissioned by the General Court of Massachusetts, and their executive, judicial and legislative power was practically supreme.[2] Eight sessions of this court were held before the meeting of the first General Court of the colony, which assembled at Hartford, May 1, 1637. Unlike the former courts, it was composed of the Magistrates, Assistants or Commissioners,[3] who had previously held such meetings, and of nine Deputies here called " Committees," three of the latter being from each of the three towns. Thus, instead of slowly working out a system of representation by a " series of expedients and compromises," the principle of democracy early asserted itself in the constitution of this " binal assembly."[4] Here we find the germs of the Senate and House of Representatives of the future State of Connecticut. They became permanently embodied in the political system of the colony by the enactment of the " Fundamental Orders " on January 1, 1638–9.[5] Under this constitution the government was organized upon a basis from which only a few permanent

---

[1] This was a newly settled town, situated so near the boundary between Massachusetts and Connecticut that it was, for several years, uncertain to which it belonged. See Palfrey, I, 235.

[2] For their commission see *Mass. Col. Rec.*, I, 170.

[3] The title of these "Magistrates" was not fixed before the Constitution of 1638–9. Dr. Bronson thinks they were chosen by the newly elected Deputies. (*Early Gov. of Conn.* in New Haven Hist. Soc. Papers, III, 297).

[4] Johnston's *Genesis of a New Eng. State*, 14, In commenting upon this assembly the author further says, " so complete are the features of Statehood, that we may fairly assign May 1, 1637, as the proper birthday of Connecticut." (*Ibid.*).

[5] This instrument, which Mr. Bryce calls "the oldest truly political Constitution in America" (*American Commonwealth*, ed. 1893, I, 429, note), provided for a government similar in all essential respects to that of Massachusetts.

departures [1] were made previous to the adoption of the constitution of 1818. The charter of 14 Charles II was practically
a royal confirmation of this instrument and, instead of altering
the government of the colony, put it on a surer footing and
extended the limits of the colonial jurisdiction.[2]

Throughout the colonial and early state history of Connecticut the Assistants were chosen from the colony as a whole
and the composition of the Council [3] remained practically
unchanged except in the number of its members.[4] During
this entire time the Governor and Deputy Governor retained
their positions as *ex officio* members of this body when acting
in every capacity; and one of them always presided when
present. Citizenship in the colony seems to have been the
only qualification for membership in this body.

The powers of the Council were, at first, confined chiefly to
the judicial and legislative departments. In the course of
time, however, it entered more fully upon the executive
domain. The wording of the Fundamental Orders clearly
indicates that its framers, who were fresh from the conflicts
that had been so fiercely waged between the patricians and the

---

[1] Although, as is well known, Andros failed to take away the charter of
Connecticut, he took the government into his hands in 1687. But upon
his imprisonment in 1689 the old officers, after an interruption of nineteen
months, resumed their duties according to the charter. (*Conn. Col. Rec.*,
III, 250; Palfrey, II, 384–5; Turnbull's *Hist. of Conn.*, I, 376–7).

[2] Loomis and Calhoun, 104–5. This charter is almost an exact reproduction of the Massachusetts charter of 1628, with an additional provision
recognizing a representative system. It led to the absorption of the New
Haven colony and the loss of all its characteristic institutions. (Atwater's
Hist. of New Haven, 520–7). Hence the history of this colony demands no
consideration in this connection.

[3] This term is used in anticipation of the subsequent history of this body,
since it does not appear in the records before those who had been called
"Magistrates" in the Fundamental Orders (*Conn. Col. Rec.*, I, 21) and
"Assistants" in the charter (*Ibid.*, II, 4) came to acquire executive power.

[4] According to the Fundamental Orders it consisted of at least six members while the charter required a membership of at least twelve.

plebs of the mother colony, were still disposed to regard the
Magistrates with a high degree of jealousy and suspicion.[1]

Section II.—*The Executive Function.*

In no part of the Fundamental Orders was this predilection
shown more clearly than in the limitations placed upon the
exercise of the modicum of executive power, which it granted
this body. To be sure, "the Gou'nor and the gretest p'te of
the Magestrats" were given power to convene the General
Court in either regular or special sessions;[2] but it was also
provided that in case they should "neglect or refuse to call
the two Generall standing Courts or ether of thē, as also at
other tymes when the occasions of the Cōmonwealth" required,
"the Freemen . . . or the Mayor p'te of them" were given
power to petition to them "soe to do;" and "if then yt be
ether denyed or neglected" this power could be exercised by
the freemen themselves.[3]

In the course of time, however, this jealousy was somewhat
allayed, and at the General Court of March, 1662–3, "the
Assistants . . . on the Riuer" were given power to act in "y[e]
vacancy of the sitting of the Generale Court" "in all necessary
concernments, both miletary and civile, according as the p'sent
exegents require and call for."[4] Before that time specific
matters pertaining to the executive function of the government[5] were often referred to the Particular Court of Assistants,
or to individual Magistrates,[6] but they had never before been
authorized to act in *all* "necessary concernments." Although

---

[1] Dr. Bronson (*Early Gov. of Conn.*—New Haven Hist. Soc. Papers, III,
318) observes that these people "had witnessed the struggle in Massachusetts
between the aristocratic and republican members of the government . . .
were on the popular side and took effectual measures to circumscribe patri-
cian ambition."

[2] Orders 6 and 10.　　　[3] *Ibid.*　　　[4] *Conn. Col. Rec.*, I, 397.
[5] *Ibid.*, I, 397.　　　[6] *Ibid.*, 71, 255, 277, etc.

this order was repealed in April, 1665,[1] the Governor and the Assistants still continued to perform executive duties in the intervals of the General Court.[2] In July, 1675, executive power was granted to the Governor, Deputy Governor and Assistants with four other persons.[3] Similar councils were constituted from time to time,[4] until May, 1677, when the membership of the Executive Council was, for the first time, restricted to the Governor, Deputy Governor and the whole body of Assistants.[5] It remained unchanged in composition until the usurpation of Andros. After that time it varied greatly as to its powers and composition, though the right of any of the Assistants to membership in the Executive Council was never denied.[6]

In the answers of the General Court to the queries of the Lords of the Committee of Colonies given in July, 1680, the powers and the composition of the Standing Council are thus stated : " As there is any special occasion the Governor calls his Assistants, who are his Council, to meet and consider of such matters as fall in the interval of the General Courts, and determine the same." [7]

In the latter part of the colonial period many powers which had been formerly delegated to the Council came to be exercised by the Governor alone.[8] Thus at a comparatively early date there began to appear indications of an evolutionary process which ultimately resulted in a complete absorption of the executive function by the Governor.

---

[1] *Ibid.*, 94, 188, 316, etc.

[2] *Ibid.*, 440. The records contain the proceedings of as many as three such meetings between the 1st and 9th of July, 1675, the date when the Council was revived. See *Ibid.*, II, 331 *et seq.*

[3] *Ibid.*, 261.   [4] *Ibid.*, 284, 289.   [5] *Ibid.*, 316-7.

[6] Unlike the Council of the mother colony, that of Connecticut was strictly subordinate to the General Assembly and was dependent upon that body for all its powers and even for its very existence.

[7] *Conn. Col. Rec.*, III, 294 ; Chalmers' *Annals*, 307.

[8] Cf. *Conn. Col. Rec.*, VIII, 87, 376, with X, 350, 424, 461, 485, 550 ; VIII, 326, with X, 348, XI, 99, 126, 234, 354, 486, XIV, 430 ; VII, 77-8, VIII, 440, 461, with X, pp. 483-4, etc.

Section III.—The Judicial Function.

At the beginning of the government of Connecticut, the judicial duties and powers of the Counsellors extended to all the tribunals that existed in the colony previous to the granting of the charter. As in Massachusetts, they were not limited to the general judicial authority which they performed as members of the General Court.[1] They also exercised judicial power in the Particular Court,[2] which from 1638 to 1665 constituted the highest strictly judicial tribunal in the colony.[3]

Upon the reorganization of the government of the colony under the charter, several important changes were made in the judicial system in order to meet the needs of an increased population and an extended territory.

---

[1] In both colonies the legislative body received not only the name but the authority of a judicial tribunal. This power cannot be said to have been completely surrendered by this body until the formation of the constitution of 1818. In 1726 an appeal to the King in Council was refused John Winthrop because he had not previously referred his case to the Assembly as the Supreme Court of the colony. (*Conn. Col. Rec.*, VII, 20). From time to time, however, appeals to the General Assembly became so numerous that various expedients were resorted to in order to restrict them. See Loomis and Calhoun, 106–7, 132.

[2] *Conn. Col. Rec.*, I, 21. It was composed at first of the Governor or Deputy Governor and a majority of Magistrates, but after May, 1647, the Governor, or Deputy Governor and two Magistrates were empowered to hold its sessions. It met four times a year and tried all cases of appeal from the lower courts and all other causes exceeding forty shillings. At first all causes were tried by a jury which seems to have been in attendance from the first institution of this court. (Trumbull, I, 125). After February, 1644, causes under forty shillings were tried by the Magistrates without a jury (*Conn. Col. Rec.*, I, 118, 535), and in cases when juries were employed, the Magistrates were granted great discretionary power in affixing penalties (*Ibid.*, 138, 324), and they were even allowed to set aside the verdict of a jury when, according to their judgment, it was unjust (*Conn. Col. Rec.*, I, 117, 118); and to decide all cases whereon the jury disagreed (*Ibid.*, 85). After March, 1662–3, persons convicted before this Court "for a misdemeanor" were allowed an appeal to the General Court (*Ibid.*, 395). See also Loomis and Calhoun, 126–7.

[3] *Memorial Hist. of Hartford County*, I, 109.

3

The General Court, or General Assembly as it was then called, still exercised judicial power and, in fact, continued to do so, to a greater or less degree, until the formation of the constitution of 1818.

The powers which had been exercised by the Particular Court were divided between two newly created tribunals,—the County Courts and the Court of Assistants. From 1666 to 1698 the County Courts[1] consisted of one Assistant, or "as we would now say Senator,"[2] and at least two Commissioners or of any three Assistants.[3] In 1698, however, the Assistants ceased to be *ex officio* members of these tribunals,[4]—this being the first instance of a diminution in the judicial powers of this body during its process of evolution into a Senate.

In October, 1665, the Court of Assistants succeeded the Particular Court as the highest strictly judicial body in the colony.[5] The membership of this new court was also confined to the Governor, or Deputy Governor and Magistrates, who at this time came to be called Assistants.[6] It existed until 1711[7]

---

[1] The first County Court was established in May, 1665, for the New Haven colony, which had just lost its General Court. (Trumbull, I, 276-7). A similar court was also established at New London at the same date. (*Ibid.*). In October of the same year a similar court was established for Hartford (*Conn. Col. Rec.*, II, 29), and the next year they were established for all the counties of the colony. (*Ibid.*, 35). They were composed at first of two Assistants and three Justices of the Quorum. (Trumbull, I, 276-7).

[2] *Memorial Hist. of Hartford County*, I, 110.   [3] *Conn. Col. Rec.*, II, 35.

[4] After 1698 they were composed of one judge and from two to five Justices of the Peace and Quorum. The jurisdiction of these courts, while composed of Assistants, extended to all cases, both civil and criminal, except those involving life, limb, or banishment. Causes involving more than twenty shillings were tried by a jury.

[5] *Conn. Col. Rec.*, II, 28-9.

[6] *Ibid.; Memorial Hist. of Hartford County*, I, 113; Loomis and Calhoun, 129. It was empowered to meet twice a year, to hear and determine appeals from the lower courts and to try capital offences and crimes respecting life, limb, or banishment. Appeals were tried by a jury "if the nature of the case required." (*Conn. Col. Rec.*, II, 29; III, 294; Chalmers, 307). It was also granted jurisdiction in cases of divorce and the powers of a Court of Admiralty. (Loomis and Calhoun, 129).

[7] Owing to a typographical error, Loomis and Calhoun (p. 131) give 1811 as the date of this change.

when it was succeeded by the Superior Court of the colony, both of which had practically the same composition and power. In 1784 an act was passed by the General Assembly declaring that the office of judge of this court was incompatible with membership in the Assembly, or in the Congress of the United States.[1] This seems to have been the second instance in which the judicial powers of the Senate were limited in the process of its evolution into a strictly legislative body.

In 1784 a Superior Court of Errors was established. It consisted of the Governor, Lieutenant Governor[2] and Assistants.[3] The defects in the composition of this tribunal soon became apparent,—since its membership was determined with reference to the position the Assistants were to hold in the General Assembly, which was the larger and more important body.[4] The Assistants were chosen because of their qualifications as legislators, rather than judges, hence the judicial system felt the evil effects of this law. It was therefore repealed in 1806, and from that date this tribunal was composed of the several judges of the Superior Court instead of the Senators serving in an *ex officio* capacity.[5] This was the third and last step in limiting the judicial powers of the Senate previous to the adoption of the Constitution of 1818.

---

[1] Loomis and Calhoun, 133.

[2] Loomis and Calhoun (p. 133) say that the Governor became a member of this tribunal in 1793, while *Memorial Hist. of Hartford County* (I, p. 113) gives this date as the time when the Lieutenant Governor was admitted to it.

[3] This court was held at first annually, alternating between Hartford and New Haven. In 1801 it was enacted that this body should consist of six members and was to hold two sessions in each county annually, one in summer and the other in winter. (Loomis and Calhoun, pp. 133–4). Its jurisdiction extended to all cases which had previously gone before the General Assembly by writ of error. Civil actions had been excluded from the General Assembly since May, 1697. (*Conn. Col. Rec.*, IV, 200).

[4] Loomis and Calhoun, 133–4.

[5] *Ibid.;* Pease and Niles' *Gazetteer of Conn. and R. I.*, ed. 1819, 18.

,

Section IV.—*The Legislative Function.*

Legislative authority was vested solely in the General Court or Assembly,[1] which was composed of two branches,—the upper consisting of the Magistrates or Assistants[2] elected by the freemen at large and the lower of Deputies, or Representatives chosen by the several towns. They occupied the same chamber and were presided over by the Governor, or Deputy Governor, or in the absence of both by a Moderator.[3] Two sessions of this court were held annually. The fall term was for the " making of laws," while the spring term was for the election of officers, after which it might " proceed in any public service as at other. courts."[4] Each session, however, embraced many meetings, which were adjourned from time to time and thus extended over a period of several months. The legislative power of this court extended over the whole colony and was practically unrestricted.[5]

It was found necessary to make only a few changes in the privileges of the two branches of the General Court and in their relations to each other. For the first six years after the organization of the government, the two branches sat together and voted as one body. Of course, this gave a great advantage to the larger branch. After the lapse of six years, however, the prejudice against the Magistrates, as shown in the Fundamental Orders, had abated to such an extent that the Deputies were willing to make a heroic sacrifice of the advantage they

---

[1] *Conn. Col. Rec.,* III, 295.

[2] Dr. Bronson (*Early Government of Conn.*—New Haven Hist. Soc. Papers, III, 317) judging by the wording of the Fundamental Orders and by the state of mind of its framers, thinks that the granting of legislative power to the Magistrates was " an after-thought" and that "it is not in harmony with the other parts of the Constitution."

[3] *Conn. Col. Rec.,* II, 24–5.   [4] *Ibid.,* 22.

[5] Loomis and Calhoun, 103. The charter forbade the enacting of laws "contrary to the laws and statutes of the realm of England," but no provision was made for its enforcement. (Palfrey, II, 41).

held over the minority. On February 5, 1644–5, an act was passed granting to each body "a negative voice" upon the actions of the other.[1] This "important concession on the part of the popular majority" was the first instance in which separate rights were accorded to each body. The passage of this act was probably due to the combined influence of the mother colony, which had just introduced the bicameral system,[2] and the "increasing weakness of the aristocratic party in England."[3] In 1724 it became necessary to make an exception to it in the election of Governor.[4]

The second step in the evolution of the Council as a legislative body was taken in October, 1698, when it was enacted that the General Court, or Assembly which had hitherto constituted a unicameral body should be divided into two separate branches, the first of which was to consist of the Governor, or Deputy Governor and Assistants, and was to be "known by the name of the Upper House."[5] The Governor was not given a veto power, but, as President of the Council, was allowed a casting vote in case the vote of that body should be equally divided.[6] Any bill could originate in either house but was not allowed to have the force of law without the concurrence of the other. This act was put into execution at the next meeting of the Assembly, held in May, 1699.[7] No subsequent change was made in the rights and functions of the Upper House nor in its relations to the popular branch during the colonial and early state history of Connecticut. This colony did not follow the example of most of the other colonies and

---

[1] *Conn. Col. Rec.*, I, 119.   [2] See *supra*.   [3] Bronson, 321.
[4] *Conn. Col. Rec.*, VI, 415, note, 483–4. Other officers were still chosen by the two bodies sitting apart. (*Ibid.*, 377).
[5] *Ibid.*, IV, 267, 282; Trumbull, I, 399; Palfrey, III, 208; Loomis and Calhoun, 106.
[6] Douglass, *Summary*, II, 168.
[7] *Conn. Col. Rec.*, IV, 282. On this subject see also Prof. T. F. Moran's *Rise and Development of the Bicameral System in America*, J. H. U. Studies, Thirteenth Series, V, 16–22.

adopt a new constitution upon emerging into statehood, but continued its government after the ancient form, a statute being enacted the session after the memorable 4th of July, 1776, which provided that the government should continue to be organized and administered according to the provisions of the charter.[1]

Section V.—The Constitution of 1818.

The final step in the process of evolution was taken upon the formation of the first state constitution in 1818. It provided for the definitive separation of the three functions of government.[2] The executive and judicial powers of the Council were taken away and the body was erected into a true Senate.[3] Its membership remained the same in number[4] and was still chosen from the State at large.[5] There was, however, a change as to its composition. Owing to the separation of

---

[1] Pease and Niles' *Gazetteer of Conn. and R. I.*, 18. The changes occasioned by the transition from colony to state were very slight. In 1775 the regnal year disappeared from the head of the records. (*Conn. Col. Rec.*, XV, 185, note). In June, 1776, acts were purported to be passed by the "General Court or Assembly of the English Colony of Connecticut in New England," while in October of the same year they were said to be by the "State of Connecticut in New England." (*Memorial Hist. of Hartford County*, I, 107).

Instead of forming a new constitution the inhabitants of Connecticut contented themselves with their old charter of 1662, to which they merely prefixed a Bill of Rights. This Bill of Rights (Paragraph I) begins as follows: " *Be it enacted and declared by the Governor, and Council, and House of Representatives, in General Court assembled*, That the ancient Form of Civil Government, contained in the Charter from *Charles* the Second, King of *England*, and adopted by the People of this State, shall be and remain the Civil Constitution of this State, under the sole authority of the People thereof, independent of any King or Prince whatever."

[2] Articles II; X, Sec. 4.   [3] Article II, Sec. 1.

[4] Cf. Article III, Sec. 4, with *Conn. Col. Rec.*, II, 5.

[5] Article III, Secs. 5–6. A change was made in this feature of the constitution by an amendment ratified in November, 1828, which required the choice of Senators according to districts. (Amendments to the Constitution of 1818, Art. II).

governmental functions, the Governor, who now became the chief executive of the State,[1] no longer retained his seat as an *ex officio* member of the Senate,[2] and the Lieutenant Governor succeeded to the position of president of that body, a duty which he had always performed in the absence of the Governor.[3] The casting vote which had been accorded the presiding officer in the Council was still retained,[4] and the veto power of the Governor was introduced for the first time in the history of the State.[5]

---

[1] Article IV, Sec. 1.
[2] The only qualification for membership in this body seems to have been citizenship within the State.
[3] Article IV, Sec. 13.
[4] Cf. Article IV, Sec. 13, with *Conn. Col. Rec.*, I, 25.
[5] Article IV, Sec. 12.

CHAPTER III.

NEW HAMPSHIRE.

Section I.—Governmental Beginnings.

The inhabitants of the little settlements along the several branches of the Piscataqua learned their first political lessons from Massachusetts, under whose jurisdiction they spent thirty-eight years at the very beginning of their governmental career.[1] The laws, customs and institutions of Massachusetts were quickly adopted in New Hampshire, and the two colonies soon became one in sympathy and in governmental policy.

On September 18, 1679, Charles II issued a commission[2] which separated the two colonies and erected, what Douglass calls the "insignificant colony"[3] of New Hampshire, into a distinct province with a separate President and Council. This change went into effect January 1, 1680, at which date the history of the Council of New Hampshire properly begins.[4]

---

[1] By virtue of an instrument signed by five inhabitants of these settlements on April 14, 1641, the people of New Hampshire came to enjoy the same liberties and administration of justice as those of Massachusetts. (*New Hampshire Provincial Papers*, I, 156–9; Farmer's Belknap's *Hist. of N. H.*, 30; Hubbard, 372). The government of this section had previously consisted of four distinct voluntary associations, which were liable to be further subdivided over the disagreements that are inevitable in political affairs.

[2] *Prov. Papers*, I, 373; Poore's *Charters and Constitutions*, II, 1275.

[3] *Summary of America*, II, 34.

[4] During the union with Massachusetts, New Hampshire was entitled to only two Deputies, no mention being made of any representation in the Council. See *Prov. Papers*, I, 159; Farmer's Belknap, 31; Savage's Winthrop, II, 92.

40

Several changes were made in the government of the colony previous to the outbreak of the Revolution,[1] yet the history of the Council, with one slight exception,[2] extends throughout this entire period of ninety-five years.

Its members were never chosen by the people in their annual elections, as was the case in the neighboring colonies, but were appointed by the Crown.[3] They cannot, therefore, be said to have constituted an independent body at any time in the colonial period. They were always selected from the colony as a whole, without regard to the interests of the different sections,[4] and could be dismissed by the President at his discretion.[5]

During the entire colonial period the powers of this body were threefold—executive, judicial and legislative. The extent of its effective authority, however, was greatly modified by such arbitrary rulers as Cranfield, Barefoot and Andros.

Section II.—The Executive Function.

The Council had no executive powers independent of the Governor, or in his absence of the Lieutenant Governor, both

---

[1] It remained a separate royal province from 1680 to 1686, when it became a province of New England. Upon the overthrow of Andros in 1690 it again united with Massachusetts. This union lasted until 1692, when it again became a separate royal province. In 1699 another change was made by which it was partially united with Massachusetts, each colony having the same Governor, but different Lieutenant Governors, Councils and Assembly of Representatives. In 1741 it became a separate royal province for the third time and remained as such until 1775.

[2] The second union with Massachusetts (1690–92) was made on the same basis as the first. Hence New Hampshire had no representation in the Council. See *supra.* Cf. *Prov. Papers,* I, 156–9, with *Ibid.,* II, 35–6.

[3] In Cutts' Commission, six out of the ten Counsellors were appointed by the King. (*N. H. Hist. Coll.,* VIII, 2; *Prov. Papers,* I, 375; Poore, II, 1275). In subsequent commissions the King retained the power to appoint all Counsellors except when the number fell below seven at any one time. (*Prov. Papers,* I, 435; II, 58, 306, 367–8, and VI, 909–10).

[4] This finally became a source of complaint on the part of the representatives.

[5] In Cranfield's Commission those who had been thus dismissed were ineligible to a seat in the Assembly. (*Prov. Papers,* I, 435).

of whom were *ex officio* members of it when acting in such a
capacity.[1] Its executive sessions were held so often at Portsmouth,[2] at or near which a majority generally resided, that it
finally came to be the only recognized place of meeting.[3] The
Governor and Council could convene the legislative assembly;[4]
advise as to the issuing of warrants for the disposal of public
monies;[5] build and fortify, or demolish forts, castles, cities,[6]
etc.; supervise the trade and commerce of the colony, order
fairs, markets, ports, harbors, etc.; and appoint custom-house
and warehouse officials.[7] They were also charged with the
granting of lands and tenures,[8] and the establishment of courts
of justice.[9] The last named power, though granted by the
various royal commissions, seems to have been shared from an
early date by the popular branch of the legislature regardless
of the united opposition of the Governors and the Councils.
The point was not finally conceded until 1771, when the Crown
gave the Representatives a legal basis for such action.[10]

---

[1] *Prov. Papers*, I, 370–6, 440–1; II, 63, etc.

[2] *Ibid.*, II.   [3] *Ibid.*, VII, 204.

[4] *Ibid.*, I, 379, 436; II, 58, 306, 367; VI, 910; VII, 124.

[5] *Ibid.*, I, 440; II, 65, 310, 373; VI, 912; VII, 124.

[6] *Ibid.*, I, 439; II, 60, 308, 371; VI, 911–2; VII, 124.

[7] *Ibid.*, I, 440; II, 61, 67, 311, 373; VI, 913; VII, 124.

[8] *Ibid.*, II, 310, 373; VI, 913; VII, 124.

[9] *Prov. Papers*, II, 59, 307, 369; VI, 911; VII, 124. This power was not
granted in Cutts' Commission, since the Governor and Council themselves
constituted the Court.

[10] The first contest over the exercise of this power arose in Cranfield's
administration. The wording of his commission was very vague on this
point. It reads: "We [the King] do hereby give and grant unto you
[Cranfield] full power and authority to erect, constitute and establish such
and so many courts of judicature and public justice . . . . as you and they
shall think fit and necessary." (*Prov. Papers*, I, 437.) In the copy of this
commission which was delivered to the Assembly the words, "and they"
were omitted by order of the Governor who maintained that they were
"put in by mistake." The Assembly, of course, thought that it referred
to them (*Ibid.*, 517) and demanded a voice in this matter. In the administration of Cranfield and his immediate successors, the power of the Assembly
was reduced to the minimum, but after the iniquitous rule of Andros, a

Section III.—*The Judicial Function.*

Upon the organization of the judicial system of New Hampshire after its separation from Massachusetts in 1680, the judicial business of the colony was placed for the most part into the hands of the Counsellors.

---

voice in the establishment of courts of judicature was accorded the popular branch, notwithstanding the commissions, which bestowed this entire power upon the Governor and Council. Such authority was not exercised, however, without encountering the opposition of the Council, whose rights were thus infringed upon.

In 1767 the House passed two different bills for the establishment of courts in the various counties to be created by the legislature. (*Prov. Papers*, VII, 135, 140). Both bills were rejected by the Council on the ground that such an act would be an infringement upon the prerogative of the Crown, who had vested this power in the Governor with the advice and consent of his Council. (*Ibid.*, 144). The House replied that the paragraph cited from the Governor's commission had been inserted in the first commission for erecting a government in the province and "from the exigency of affairs was then absolutely necessary till a Legal Establishment of Courts of Justice should take place; and though perhaps the same paragraph" had been inserted in all subsequent commissions, such a power had never been exercised by any Governor of the province "since the laws now in force were passed for holding said Courts in the town of Portsmouth and regulating their proceedings. In the year 1730 three of the Inferior Courts were removed from Portsmouth, one to Exeter, one to Dover, one to Hampton, and but one held at Portsmouth, but this was by an act passed for that purpose. . . . Since the year 1730 four or five Acts of Assembly have been passed for altering the times of the sitting of Courts in this Province, and we think it to be plain that the words Erect, Constitute and Establish have here an original signification of fixing those courts in the first instance." (*Ibid.*, 154-5). The Council still non-concurred. (*Ibid.*, 156, 162). The House appealed to the King (*Ibid.*, 184), who consented that the act should be passed provided it "contained a suspended clause that should not take effect till his Majesty's Pleasure should be known." (*Ibid.*, 202). Thus the point at issue was settled. The act which recognized the rights of the House to a voice in the establishment of courts of justice was passed in April, 1767 (*Ibid.*, 229), and received the royal approval in 1771. (*Ibid.*, 274, 276).

They not only exercised judicial authority in the General Court[1] as in Massachusetts, but were also constituted by the commission of President Cutts, a separate court of appeals for the whole colony. The exercise of this latter power encountered the constantly increasing opposition of the colonists from time to time. It was nevertheless renewed by subsequent commissions and instructions, and was thus continued throughout the colonial period.[2]

Three inferior courts were appointed for Dover, Hampton and Portsmouth. These were held "by ye Presid^t and Counc^{ll}, or any 6 of ye Counc^{ll} whereof ye Presid^t or his Deputy" were one "together wth a Jury of 12 honest men . . . for such as desire to be tried by a Jury."[3] There was no limit to the jurisdiction of these courts. Appeals could be taken to the King in Council on all civil cases involving over fifty pounds[4] and in "criminall cases, where ye punishm^t to be inflicted" extended "to loss of life or limb," except in "ye case of willfull murder." The individual members of the Council were also given authority to hear and determine minor offenses.[5]

---

[1] Farmer's Belknap, 222; *Prov. Papers*, I, 395. As in the other colonies, the General Assembly was usually considered the supreme tribunal for the trial of all cases of appeal from inferior courts. (*Prov. Papers*, VII, 395, *N. H. Hist. Coll.*, VIII, 22.) In Gov. Allen's instructions, however, the exercise of such power was not allowed, since appeals from the Governor and Council were expressly forbidden (*Prov. Papers*, II, 68).

[2] *N. H. Hist. Coll.*, VIII, 4.   [3] *Prov. Papers*, I, 395.

[4] *Prov. Papers*, I, 377; *N. H. Hist. Coll.*, VIII, 4.

[5] *Prov. Papers*, I, 387, 390, 392; *N. H. Hist. Coll.*, VIII, 14, 17, 19. Under the administration of Gov. Dudley New Hampshire became a county of the Province of New England and its courts were composed of Justices of the Peace and such Counsellors as might be present, one at least being required to form such a tribunal (*Prov. Papers*, I, 594). The President and Council of New England, part of which was chosen from New Hampshire, constituted the Superior Courts of Grand Assize and General Goal Delivery which held annual sessions in Boston (*Ibid.*, 595).

Andros and his Council constituted a Court of Sessions and a Superior Court of Judicature (*Ibid.*, II, 16 and 17 note; *Col. Rec. of Conn.*, III, 1678–1689), whose jurisdiction extended over New Hampshire.

The Council minutes show that in the administration of John Usher "all of ye Council" had "power as Justice of Peace in ye whole Province."

This system was in force until 1699 when the judiciary of the Colony was reorganized. Before that date, however, the courts varied greatly in character, composition and authority. At times, law and justice became "synonymous with a dictator's decrees" and Counsellors, Judges and Assemblies were dismissed with or without cause, as the Governor's prejudice determined.[1]

An act of 1699 shows a marked tendency to reduce the judicial duties of the Council as a body, since by it the Governor and Council were made a court of appeal only for civil cases involving over one hundred pounds.[2] In less than two years afterwards, the colonists made an emphatic assertion of their opposition to this tribunal. Several complaints were sent to the Queen to the effect that the Governor and Council received appeals and decided cases without taking an oath to do justice.[3] An oath was then prescribed and taken,[4] but the people were still unwilling that the Council should exercise judicial as well as executive and legislative power.[5] On January 3, 1727–8, they passed a vote "prohibiting the Sup^r Court of Judicature" from granting "appeals to the Govr & Council."[6] The Council non-concurred and cited the royal instructions as the source of its judicial authority.[7] Lieutenant Governor Wentworth put an end to the controversy by dissolving the Assembly.[8] But this did not silence the opposition

---

[1] Sanborn's *Hist. of N. H.*, 81.

[2] *Prov. Papers*, III, 86 and 220. Membership in the Council did not, however, disqualify one from exercising other judicial powers besides those pertaining to the Council as a whole.

[3] Farmer's Belknap, 222.   [4] *Prov. Papers*, II, 342.

[5] This opposition was occasioned partly because the judges who decided cases in the inferior courts were members of the Council; "partly because no jury was admitted in this court of appeal; and partly because no such institution was known in the neighboring province of Massachusetts." (Farmer's Belknap, 222).

[6] *Prov. Papers*, IV, 475.

[7] It even characterized this act as a "scandalous lible" (*Prov. Papers*, III, 480).

[8] *Ibid.*, 484.

of the people, and the existence of this tribunal was a standing grievance throughout the rest of the colonial era.[1]

Section IV.—The Legislative Function.

All the royal commissions issued to the Governor of New Hampshire vested the legislative power in the General Assembly of Representatives.[2] All the Governors except Cutts were given a veto over all the acts of the legislature.[3] All enactments passed by both houses and approved by the Governor were transmitted to the Privy Council in England and remained in force until disallowed by that authority.[4]

The first session of the General Assembly of New Hampshire met at Portsmouth on March 16, 1679–80. Profiting by the unpleasant experiences of Massachusetts, three years after they had first passed under her jurisdiction, the two branches of the Assembly sat apart[5] and it was enacted that "no Act, Imposition, Law or Ordinance be made or imposed upon" the province "but such as shall be made by the said Assembly and approved by the Presidᵗ and Councill from time to time."[6] They then proceeded to re-enact the laws of Massachusetts under which they had lived so agreeably for thirty-eight years.[7]

---

[1] In 1772 complaint was made to the Lords of Trade that the Governor and Council had deprived grantees under the crown of their lands "without any legal process" or a trial by jury (Belknap, ed. 1812, III, Appendix; Farmer's Belknap, 345; *Prov. Papers*, VII, 338).

[2] *Prov. Papers*, II, 59, 307, 369; VI, 910; VII, 124.

[3] Belknap (Farmer's Edition, 97) says that Cranfield was the first to whom such power was granted in New England.

[4] Palfrey, II, 267.

[5] See Prof. T. F. Moran's *Rise and Development of the Bicameral System in America*, J. H. U. Studies, Thirteenth Series, V, 13–16; Belknap's *Hist. of N. H.*, I, 178–9.

[6] *Prov. Papers*, I, 382–3; *N. H. Hist. Coll.*, VIII, 10.

[7] Sanborn's *Hist. of N. H.*, 78–9.

President Cutts died in 1681 and was succeeded on the following year by Edward Cranfield. Owing to Cranfield's unpopularity, in less than four months after his arrival in the colony, three members of the Council had voluntarily withdrawn and three others had been dismissed.[1] On account of a disagreement, the Assembly was dissolved by Cranfield, January 20th, 1683.[2] The Governor and Council then assumed the entire legislative authority,[3] which they retained until forced by need of money to summon a new Assembly.[4] At this session of the Assembly which convened January 14, 1684, we find the first assertion in New Hampshire of a prerogative which was claimed sooner or later by the lower house in all the colonies, except perhaps Rhode Island.[5] The Representatives rejected as "unparliamentary," a money bill which had been previously passed by the Council.[6] The Governor dissolved the Assembly on the following day,[7] and attempted to levy taxes upon his own authority.[8] Failing in this, he summoned a third Assembly six months later.[9] This Assembly also exhibited a spirit of insubordination to his demands and was likewise dismissed after a short session. From this time the right to originate money bills was never relinquished by the popular branch of the Assembly.

After the unsettled period,[10] immediately following the imprisonment of Andros[11] in 1689, Samuel Allen was appointed Governor and John Usher Lieutenant Governor of the colony. The commission[12] and instructions[13] of Governor Allen, which

---

[1] Farmer's Belknap, 98.   Two of the latter were afterwards restored.
[2] *Ibid.*   [3] *Prov. Papers*, I, 518.   [4] Farmer's Belknap, 104.
[5] See *infra.*   [6] Farmer's Belknap, 104.
[7] *Ibid.*   [8] *Ibid.*, 110.   [9] *Ibid.*
[10] From the surrender of Andros' government, April 18, 1689 (*Prov. Papers*, II, pt. I, p. 21), until the accession of Governor Allen, there was no legalized government in the colony. (*Ibid.*, 30 *et seq.*).
[11] During his administration there was no popular branch of the Legislature. Laws were made by the Governor and his Council of fifteen, only one of whom was from New Hampshire. (*Ibid.*, 118–9).
[12] *Ibid.*, 57.   [13] *Ibid.*, 63.

were issued March, 1692, constituted a frame of government, the Legislature of which was substantially the same as that provided for in the commission of President Cutts. In fact no important change was made in the legislative power of the Council throughout the rest of the colonial period.

The Assembly was held under the strict surveillance of the royal officers, and was kept too severely in check to admit of that expansion which was necessary in order to keep apace with the advancing ideas of the people. Not only was the Council at the mercy of the royal Governor, but the popular branch was held largely within the limits of his desires by his veto power and his authority to prorogue its sessions. Above them all stood the King who retained "the prerogative of disannulling the acts of the whole at his pleasure."

The last session of the General Assembly under the government of Great Britain was held July 18, 1775.[1] Previous to this date the government of the colony had been gradually assumed by representatives of the people who formed themselves into a Provincial Congress.[2] This peculiar form of government continued until January 5, 1776, when, according to the last vote of the Fifth Provincial Congress, it was decided to "take up Civil Government."[3]

Section V.—The Constitution of 1776.

This body then tried its skill at constitution-making. It first metamorphosed itself into a popular branch of the Legislature by assuming "the Name, Power & Authority of a

---

[1] *Prov. Papers*, VII, 385.

[2] Under this form of government the entire political authority of the people was delegated to a body of men who exercised executive as well as legislative power. During the recesses of this body their power was exercised by a "Committee of Safety," whose acts were as binding as those of the entire Congress.

[3] *Prov. Papers*, VIII, 2.

house of Representatives or Assembly for the Colony [1] of New Hampshire," [2] and then proceeded to create a new Council to take the place of the old one which had disappeared with the royal government. This Council, like its predecessor, constituted "a Distinct and Separate Branch of the Legislature." [3] It resembled the old Council in size and character of membership, [4] but differed from it in two respects. The new Counsellors were chosen by popular election after the expiration of the term of the first, who were appointed by the House; and they were apportioned among the different counties of the colony, [5] five being from Rockingham, two from Stafford, two from Hillsborough, two from Cheshire and one from Grafton County. [6]

This constitution did not confer any judicial authority upon the Council, as a body, independent of the Assembly; and on January 26, 1776, "All clauses " of the colonial laws " Respecting the Governor & Council Sitting or acting as a Court of Appeals " were repealed, [7] and the supreme judicial power was assumed by the legislature. [8] This act abolished the tribunal which the colonists had considered a grievance for several

---

[1] The title of "State " was not assumed until September 10, 1776. (*Prov. Papers*, VIII, 332).

[2] *Prov. Papers*, VIII, 3; *N. H. Hist. Coll.*, IV, 151–2.   [3] *Ibid.*

[4] September 19, 1776, provision was made for adding to the membership of both branches of the Legislature upon the accession of new towns or settlements. (*Prov. Papers*, VIII, 344; *N. H. Hist. Coll.*, IV, 154).

[5] *Prov. Papers.*, VIII, 3, 4; *N. H. Hist. Coll.*, IV, 153.

[6] *Prov. Papers*, VIII, 3, 6. As early as 1717 the choice of Counsellors from one locality (Portsmouth) had been made a cause for complaint on the part of the Assembly. We are told that at that time "ye whole number" of counsellors resided " w^{thin} two miles or therea^{bt} one of another." (*Prov. Papers*, III, 675). For this reason the Representatives very properly claimed at a later date, that they were better acquainted with the needs and desires of the people than were the Counsellors. (*Prov. Papers*, VII, 203–4).

[7] *Prov. Papers*, VIII, 60.

[8] A very strong plea against such an exercise of power was presented in the case of the State *vs.* Porter. (*Prov. Papers*, VIII, 327–8).

4

years.[1] With its enforcement the Council as a body ceased to exercise judicial powers, but its members still served in an *ex officio* judicial capacity as individuals.[2]

One of the greatest defects of the hastily formed Constitution of 1776 was the want of an executive branch of government. To remedy this the two houses "of Legislature during their session performed executive as well as legislative duty," and at every adjournment a Committee of Safety was appointed to transact the business of the colony "in the recess of the General Assembly."[3] The appointment of "all civil officers for the Colony & for Each County," "Except Clerks of Courts & County Treasurers & Recorders of Deeds" was vested in both houses of the Legislature.[4] They also appointed the higher military officers who had been previously appointed by the royal Governors.[5]

No changes were made in the legislative powers of the Council. All acts and resolves "agreed to and passed by both Branches of the Legislature" had the force of law[6] and all "Bills, Resolves or votes for Raising, Levying & Collecting

[1] See *supra.*

[2] On January 12, 1776, it was voted "That the members of the Honble Council . . . be Justices of the Peace and of the Quorum throughout" the colony. (*Prov. Papers*, VIII, 18). They were also permitted to fill any other judicial office to which they might be chosen, since membership in the Council did not disqualify them for such positions. (Farmer's Belknap, 364).

[3] *Prov. Papers*, VIII, 21. The orders and recommendations of this committee had the same effect as the acts and resolves of the Council and House while in session. (*N. H. Hist. Coll.*, II, 38, note). The committeemen were chosen by the Legislature and varied in number from six to sixteen. The President of the Council was also President of the Executive Committee. (Farmer's Belknap, 364).

[4] *Prov. Papers*, VIII, 4; *N. H. Hist. Coll.*, IV, 153.

[5] *Prov. Papers*, VIII, 3, 4; *N. H. Hist. Coll.*, IV, 153.

[6] *Prov. Papers*, VIII, 3; *N. H. Hist. Coll.*, IV, 152. This rule had been observed ever since the meeting of the first General Assembly of the colony in 1679–80.

money " were still required to " Originate in the House of Representatives." [1]

Section VI.—The Proposed Constitution of 1779.[2]

This instrument proposed the following changes: (1) That the Governor with the advice of the Council be authorized to grant reprieves,[3] to call extra sessions of the General Court, and to point out the principal business of such sessions.[4] (2) That the members of the Council be disqualified from holding the office of Sheriff.[5] (3) That no member of the General Court should be judge of the Superior, the Inferior, or the Probate Court.[6] The significance of this constitution is the fact that it marks a tendency towards a separation of the functions of government.

Section VII.—The Proposed Constitution of 1781.[7]

This constitution marks another step in the development of the ideas of the people towards a separation of the functions of government which was so vaguely indicated by the proposed constitution of 1779. The executive power of the state was to be vested in the Governor and a new body to be known as the " Privy Council." [8] The former Council of twelve was to be continued under the title of " Senate," and its powers were to be restricted to the legislative function alone.[9]

---

[1] *Prov. Papers,* VIII, 3; *N. H. Hist. Coll.,* IV, 152. This power had also been exercised by the House, throughout the history of the colony.

[2] Although it was rejected by the people in their town meetings on account of its imperfections, the principal one of which was the omission of a provision for the chief executive, it nevertheless indicates certain advances in the ideas of the people as to the duties of the Council. A copy of this Constitution is given in *N. H. Hist. Coll.,* IV, 154, *et seq.*

[3] *N. H. Hist. Coll.,* IV, 160.   [4] *Ibid.,* 159.   [5] *Ibid.,* 160.   [6] *Ibid.*

[7] This constitution is not given in the *N. H. Hist. Coll.,* but the Address accompanying it which discussed its main features may be found in *Ibid.,* IV, 162–73.

[8] *N. H. Hist. Coll.,* IV, 170.   [9] *Ibid.,* 166; Farmer's Belknap, 383.

Section VIII.—*The Constitution of 1783–4.*[1]

The adoption of the second state constitution marks the final step in the evolution of the Senate in New Hampshire.

It declared that " the three essential powers " of government " ought to be kept as separate from and independent of each other as the nature of a free government will admit."[2]

The executive power was vested in the President of the state and his Council of five—two Senators and three Representatives—who were chosen annually by a joint ballot of both houses.[3]

The judicial power was exercised by officers chosen by the President and his newly created Council.[4]

The supreme legislative power was vested in a General Court composed of a Senate and a House of Representatives, each of which had " a negative on the other."[5]   The Senate was an exact counterpart of the Council under the first constitution.   It consisted of twelve persons,[6] seven of whom were necessary to constitute a quorum.   Its members were to be elected by districts ; but, until otherwise ordered by the General Court, the different counties were to elect each the

---

[1] A copy of this constitution is given in *N. H. State Papers*, XX, 9–30, and in Poore, II, 1280, *et seq.*   The convention that drew up the constitution of 1781 continued its labors for a period of more than two years (June, 1781 to October, 1783), and held no less than nine sessions.   The result of their prolonged labors is the constitution which was adopted June 2, 1784.

[2] Bill of Rights, Art. XXXVII.   The incorporation of this principle was probably due to the able arguments in the case cited above (p. 49, note 8) and to the influence of other state constitutions which embodied this feature—particularly that of Massachusetts, " which was supposed to be an improvement on all which had been framed in America."   (Farmer's Belknap, 383.)

[3] *State Papers*, XX, 24 ; Poore, II, 1289.

[4] *State Papers*, XX, 23 ; Poore, II, 1288.

[5] *State Papers*, XX, 15 ; Poore, II, 1284.

[6] Presided over by the President of the State who had a vote " equal with any other member," and also " a casting vote in case of a tie."

same number of Senators that had been granted them by the
constitution of 1776.[1]   The House still retained the power to
originate money bills, but the Senate had power to " propose
or concur with amendments as on other bills."[2]   The only
remnant of judicial power left the Senate was the trial of impeachments made by the House of Representatives,[3] as was the
case in most other states.

Senators were required to belong to the Protestant faith ; to
be possessed of a freehold estate of two hundred pounds within the State ; to be at least thirty years of age, inhabitants of
the state seven years, and, at the time of their election, inhabitants of the district from which they were chosen.[4]

---

[1] Cf. *Prov. Papers*, VIII, 3, with *State Papers*, XX, 16; Poore, II, 1285.
[2] *State Papers*, XX, 20; Poore, II, 1287.
[3] *State Papers*, XX, 18; Poore, II, 1286.   [4] *Ibid.*

CHAPTER IV.

RHODE ISLAND.

Section I.—Governmental Beginnings.

The first settlers of this state founded not a single colony, but four separate and distinct settlements; namely, Providence in 1636, Portsmouth in 1638, Newport in 1639, and Warwick in 1642.

These towns were at first independent, self-centred communities of persons who differed no less in governmental ideas [1] than in religious faith. There seems to have been, however, a

---

[1] In 1637, thirteen of the settlers of Providence signed a civil compact in which they agreed to be governed "by the maior consent of the. . . . Ihabitants maisters of families Incorporated Together into a towne fellowship and others whome they" should "admit unto them" "only in civill things." (*Early Rec. of the Town of Prov.*, I, 1; *R. I. Col. Rec.*, I, 14.) Town meetings of all the inhabitants were held monthly down to 1640, when the growth of the colony rendered a purely democratic government impracticable. (Mr. W. E. Foster's *Town Government in Rhode Island*, J. H. U. Studies, Fourth Series, II, p. 13, 16, 19; Arnold's *Hist. of the State of Rhode Island*, I, 102.) "The general business of the town" with a few exceptions, was then delegated to "5 Disposers" who held monthly meetings. They were chosen by the town meetings in which all the freemen henceforth assembled quarterly. (*R. I. Col. Rec.*, I, 108-9; *Historical Discourse* by Hon. Thomas Durfey in 250th Anniversary of Providence, 127.)

The Portsmouth settlers inclined to a sort of theocracy. Following Judaic example, they chose a Judge "to exercise authority among them." (*R. I. Col. Rec.*, I, 52.) Within a year three elders were associated with him and to them all was given "the whole care and charge of all the affairs" of the colony. They were to administer justice and to draw up such rules and laws as should be for the general welfare and "according to God." In 1639, the people discarded the theocratic element to a great extent and

54

direct line of institutional development from germs that appeared at the foundation of the two island governments, which later united, and not only took the initial step towards a union of all the settlements,[1] but furnished a model for the government of the whole colony.[2] By a rapid series of developments the Judges in the separate towns of Portsmouth and Newport

---

constituted themselves into "a civill body politicke." (*Ibid.*, 70.) The offices of Judge and Elders were continued and the number of the latter was increased to seven. Their duties as a body seem to have been confined principally to the judicial function, and a jury system was introduced. (*Ibid.*)

The government of Newport was a counterpart of that of Portsmouth, from which it sprang, and with which it was finally united. It also had Judges and Elders (*Ibid.*, 87) who served chiefly in a judicial capacity (*Ibid.*, 90, 93), though they were granted some executive power. (*Ibid.*, 95). In legislative power they do not seem to have been superior to other freemen who attended the General Quarter Courts.

In 1640 Portsmouth and Newport united in a common government. (*Ibid.*, 100). The titles of "Judge" and "Elder" were then abolished by the General Court and those of "Governor" and "Assistant" substituted in their stead. Provision was made for the election of a Governor, a Deputy Governor and four Assistants, the Governor and two Assistants to be chosen in one town and the Deputy and two other Assistants in the other town. · (*Ibid.*, 101). They were "invested with the offices of Justices of the Peace" *ex officio*. At the next "General Courte," "particular Courts" consisting of "Magistrates (Assistants) and Jurors" were established to be held each month at Newport and Portsmouth alternately for the trial of "all such cases and actions as shall be presented." (*Ibid.*, 103). Three months later the Magistrates of each town were constituted a tribunal for the trial of all cases, matters of life and death only excepted, that might arise in their respective towns.

The settlers at Warwick, under the influence of Gorton, maintained that they had no legal right to erect a government without being authorized to do so by the mother country. (*Ibid.*, 129). They therefore remained without any form of government until the organization of the colonial government in 1647.

[1] *R. I. Col. Rec.*, I, 125; Arnold, I, 113.

[2] Providence instructed its commissioners who attended the first meeting of the towns under the charter of 1663–4 "to hold correspondency with the whole in that model that hath been lately shown unto us by our worthy friends of the Island." (*R. I. Col. Rec.*, I, 43; Staples' *Annals*, R. I. Hist. Soc. Coll., Vol. V, 62).

were succeeded by the Governor of the united government of the island, and then the President of the whole colony under the first charter.[1] The Elders at the same time and by a similar course of evolution became the Magistrates or Assistants of the island and then of the united colony.[2] The history of their development into a Senate is unique. They came into existence as a purely executive and judicial body, but later acquired legislative power without losing their authority in the other branches of government. They finally lost their executive and judicial functions, but retained legislative power, and thus became a true Senate.

On March 14, 1643–4, the English Parliamentary Commission granted a charter or patent[3] to Providence, Newport and Portsmouth[4] under the name of the Providence Plantations.[5]

---

[1] This charter was formed upon the Massachusetts model, with an additional feature which provided for a representative system, similar to that which had grown up in Massachusetts. All the New England colonies were assimilated to the same model.

[2] See *supra*.

[3] There seems to be no ground for the distinction between a charter and a patent as given in Jameson's *Dictionary of American History*, p. 124. That grants to individuals were not always called patents is evident from the wording of the instruments granted to Lord Baltimore (Poore's *Charters and Constitutions*, I, 811–17) and to William Penn (*Ibid.*, II, 1509–15). On the other hand the words, "charter" and "patent," seem to have been indiscriminately used to designate grants both to corporations and to individuals. See *R. I. Col. Rec.*, II, 143–6; *Conn. Col. Rec.*, I, 384. In fact, no distinctions seem to have been made, by the colonists at least, in the use of these terms. Penn referred to his "charter" of 1681 as "Letters Patent." (Poore's *Charters and Constitutions*, II, 1536). See also Jacob's *Law Dictionary* (London, 1809) under titles "Charters of Private Persons," "Grants of the King," and "Patents," and Black's *Law Dic.*, pp. 196, 877.

[4] Although Warwick was not mentioned in the charter, it united with the other towns at the organization of the government of the colony.

[5] A copy of this charter may be found in *R. I. Col. Rec.*, I, 143–6; *Coll. of R. I. Hist. Soc.*, IV, 221–5; and Poore's *Charters and Constitutions*, II, 1594–5. An excellent account of the "Origin of the Charter Government and Its Fundamental Principles" may be found in Burke's Report on "*Rhode Island—Interference of the Executive in the affairs of*," (Pub. Doc., 28th Congress, 1st Session. House Representatives Report No. 546) 6–8.

It prescribed no form of government nor mode of organization. In fact, it still left the towns independent of each other and was calculated to produce a confederation (*Staatenbund*) rather than a union (*Bundestaat*).[1]

After the lapse of more than three years from the granting of the charter, the first General Assembly of the colony met at Portsmouth. The charter was then formally adopted and the government systematically organized. The executive and judicial powers were largely vested in a President and four Assistants,[2] the latter of whom were annually elected by the freemen of the several towns. A novel method of making laws was then devised, by which the legislative power was made to reside ultimately in the people.[3] This cumbersome

---

[1] Staples' *Annals*, 68; Arnold's *Hist. of R. I.*, I, 285. The charter granted the inhabitants "full Power and Authority to rule themselves" "by such a Form of Civil Government as by voluntary consent of all or the greater Part of them, they shall find most suitable to their Estate and Condition." (*R. I. Col. Rec.*, I, 145).

[2] Chalmers' *Annals* 273. They were given power "to arrest and bail out or imprison all disturbers of the peace" (*R. I. Col. Rec.*, I, 192-3); and under certain circumstances, to issue summons (*Ibid.*, 340-1), grant commissions (*Ibid.*, 347), and call special sessions of the General Assembly (*Ibid.*, 276).

As a judicial tribunal they were granted power "to hold semi-annually the General Court of Tryall for the whole Colonie." (*Ibid.*, 191, 194-5.) "This court was held semi-annually and its jurisdiction extended over all matters of greater weight," such as the higher class of crimes, cases between town and town, between citizens and strangers; and in general, to all matters "not referred to other tribunals." (Durfee's *Gleanings from the Judicial Hist. of R. I.*, 7, 8, Pub. in R. I. Hist. Tracts, No. 18.) In 1651, this tribunal was "converted into a court of appeal or review." (*Ibid.*)

They were also made "conservators of the peace in the Towne where they live and throwout the whole Colony" (*R. I. Col. Rec.*, I, 192), and were authorized to act as Coroner in each town where they dwelt. (*Ibid.*, 195.)

[3] Any town of the colony could take the initiative in legislation. When a town desired the enactment of a law which concerned the whole colony, the bill was drawn up, discussed and voted upon in the town-meeting. If it was favorably considered by this meeting, a copy of the proposed law was sent to the other towns for similar consideration. A report of the actions of all the towns was then 'commended' to the "Committee for the

method, however, was forsaken after a brief trial and the legislative power came to be largely exercised by a "Committee" of six from each of the towns. ˙

The second charter, which was granted in 1663, marks the entrance of the Assistants upon the legislative domain. It vested the government of the colony in a Governor, Deputy Governor, ten Assistants,[1] and eighteen Deputies.[2] The

---

General Courte"—a body composed of six from each town. If it was found that "the major parte of the Colonie" concurred in the bill it was declared "a Law till the next Generall Assembly of all the people" should determine whether or not it should continue longer. In all cases where the Assembly took the initiative in legislation, the bill as passed by that body was referred by the Committee to the different towns, where it was voted on by the people. These votes were sent "by the Towne Clarke of each Towne . . . . to the General Recorder," who, in the presence of the President opened and counted them. If a majority of the votes were favorable to the bill it stood "as a law till the next General Assemblie" when it was either confirmed or annulled. (*R. I. Col. Rec.*, I, 148–9; Staples' *Annals*, 65.) The Committee gradually assumed legislative authority under the title of "the Court of Commissioners" until they came to be in fact the General Assembly, although others who desired might sit with them. (*R. I. Col. Rec.*, I, 213, 228, 277; Arnold, 1, 219.) Having assumed the authority of the General Assembly they then assumed that title. (Arnold, I, 230.) A limit was also made to the time when the towns might interpose their objections to acts initiated by the General Assembly, which acts otherwise became laws. (*R. I. Col. Rec.*, I, 229, 401, 429.) The referendum was finally abolished under the second charter (*R. I. Col. Rec.*, II, 26) and in 1672 speaking "against any of the Acts and Orders" of the Assembly "at any time, more especially in any town meeting," etc., was made a crime punishable "at the discretion of the Justices." (*Ibid.*, 439.)

[1] Of the twelve State Officers—two Executives and ten Assistants—five were required to be inhabitants of Newport, three of Providence and two each of Portsmouth and Warwick. (*R. I. Col. Rec.*, II, 33; Staples' *Annals*, 141; Arnold, I, 302). This appears to have been the first instance in New England, and probably in any of the colonies, in which the Counsellors were distributed according to geographical location. An act which was passed in Massachusetts in the administration of Governor Phipps (1694), requiring all Deputies to be residents of the district they represented, is often incorrectly cited as the first instance in which this principle was introduced in the American colonies.

[2] Newport was allowed six Deputies and the three remaining towns four each. Towns that might be subsequently added were to be allowed two Deputies each.

Assistants were elected annually and represented the colony as a whole, while the Deputies were elected semi-annually [1] and represented the towns.

Section II.—The Executive Function.

This charter granted the Governor or Deputy Governor and Assistants authority over the militia, whenever occasion might arise in a recess of the General Assembly.[2] This proved a very important and timely provision, since ample occasion soon arose for the exercise of such power. Beginning in May, 1667, the Governor and Council,—for such it had become in name [3]—held frequent meetings in the intervals of the General Assembly.[4] This became necessary because of a threatened invasion by the French and Dutch, with whom the mother country was at enmity, and the rapidly developing hostility of the Indians which finally culminated in King Philip's War. . Their charter powers were amplified by the General Assembly which authorized them to raise and equip troops ; to order their movements ; to appoint and commission officers ; and in short, to take all necessary steps for defending the colony, if occasion should arise.[5] In the exercise of these duties, their acts were considered equally binding with those of the Assembly.[6] In 1669 they arranged for monthly meetings of the Council,[7] but the condition of affairs rendered it necessary

---

[1] The origin of semi-annual elections of Deputies probably dated back to the act of the first General Assembly of the colony (1647) by which the representative system was created. It provided that "a week before any General Courte," which met twice a year, " notice should be given to every Towne by the head officers that they chuse a Committee for the Transaction of the affairs there." (*R. I. Col. Rec.*, I, 147).

[2] *R. I. Col. Rec.*, II, 14; Douglass' *Summary*, II, 85.

[3] Within a year of the granting of the charter, the Assistants, while acting in an executive capacity, assumed the title of "Council." (*R. I. Col. Rec.*, II, 67).

[4] *Ibid.*, 191 *et seq.*   [5] *Ibid.*, 205–8, 212.
[6] Arnold, I, 330.   [7] *R. I. Col. Rec.*, II, 256.

to assemble much more frequently.[1] Their summary dealings
with Ninecraft,[2] their effective action in the King's Province
dispute,[3] their prompt announcement of the royal proclama-
tions[4] and their power to treat with enemies[5] and to appoint
town officers,[6] indicate the nature and extent of their executive
authority from time to time. In October, 1708, we find that
no war measures at all were taken by the General Assembly.[7]
This was probably due to the fact that sufficient power had
already been granted the Council to provide for defence against
the enemy.[8]

By the outbreak of the Revolutionary War, however, the
Council had almost ceased to exercise executive power as a
body. The matters which arose in the recess of the Assembly
were entrusted to special committees appointed by that body
when occasion arose. These committees varied in name[9] and
composition[10] from time to time, but their general powers were
the same as those that had been previously exercised by the
Governor and Council.

Section III.—*The Judicial Function.*

" The charter," says Judge Durfee, " did not *create* judicial
tribunals, but empowered the General Assembly to create
them ; and accordingly, the General Assembly, at its first
session under the charter," turned its attention to a reorganization of the judicial system.[11] The Assistants were given power

---

[1] Arnold, I, 338.
[2] *R. I. Col. Rec.*, II, 264–6, 269; Arnold, I, 339 *et seq.*
[3] *R. I. Col. Rec.*, II, 256, 298; Arnold, I, 338, 344–6.
[4] *R. I. Col. Rec.*, II, 461–2; Arnold, I, 359.
[5] *R. I. Col. Rec.*, II, 489–90.   [6] *Ibid.*, III, 89.
[7] *Ibid.*, IV, 48 *et seq.*   [8] Arnold, II, 34.
[9] They were called " Committees of Safety," " Recess Committees," and
" Councils of War."
[10] *R. I. Col. Rec.*, VII, 327, 365, 383, 543; VIII, 22, 56, 229, 316, 419, 422,
471–2, 545, 616, etc.
[11] *Gleanings, etc.*, 11 ; *R. I. Col. Rec.*, I, 25 *et seq.*

greater even than they had exercised under the first charter. In fact, they seem to have been granted almost a monopoly of judicial authority, since they not only served in this capacity as individuals,[1] but they also constituted as a body, four of the most important tribunals in the colony.[2]

They were required to hold "a special Court or Courts in Newport for merchants and seamen, or any other," when occasion arose;[3] also semi-annual "Courts of Triall" alternately at Providence and Warwick "for the trial of any actional matter to the value of and under ten pounds, debt or damages."[4] Matters referred to these courts finally passed into the jurisdiction of the county courts upon the division of the colony into counties."[5]

The General Court of Trials as constituted under the first charter was continued under the second, though there was an alteration in its composition and place of meeting. Its membership was confined exclusively to the Governor, Deputy Governor, and at least six Assistants,[6] and its sessions were held semi-annually at Newport.[7] In 1729 its name was changed to "The Superior Court of Judicature, Court of As-

---

[1] They were *ex officio* members of the town councils (*R. I. Col. Rec.*, II, 27 ; Douglass' *Summary*, II, 85 ; Staples' *Annals*, 140, 155, 172) and served as Coroners in the towns where they lived. (*R. I. Col. Rec.*, II, 28).

[2] These were : (1), The special courts for Newport; (2), Two semi-annual courts for Providence and Warwick ; (3), The General Courts of Trial ; (4), Probate Courts with only an appellate jurisdiction. They also constituted the Court for King's Province until 1669. (*R. I. Col. Rec.*, II, 256).

[3] *R. I. Col. Rec.*, II, 26–7.   [4] *Ibid.*, 31.

[5] For the extent of jurisdiction exercised by the county courts, the justices of the peace, the General Sessions of the Peace and the Inferior Courts of Common Pleas, see Acts and Laws of R. I. from 1745 to 1750, ed. 1752, 77, 110; *R. I. Col. Rec.*, V ; Douglass' *Summary*, II, 95–96.

[6] Under the charter of 1643–4 this court was composed at first of the Governor and Assistants, but in May, 1649, the Magistrates of the town where the court assembled for the time, were added to the tribunal. (*R. I. Col. Rec.*, I, 218).

[7] Under the former charter this court was required to be held at the different towns of the colony in succession.

size and General Goal Delivery," and its jurisdiction became
more largely appellate in both civil and criminal matters,[1] but
its composition and place of meeting,—two of its most radical
defects under the second charter,[2]—remained unchanged. But
with the increase of litigation consequent upon the increase of
population, the Assembly was finally forced to remedy these
defects. The change was made in 1747 by an act which required that in lieu of the Governor or Deputy Governor and
Assistants, this court should be held by five judges,[3] a chief
and four associates who were to be appointed annually by the
General Court.[4] Although this act excluded the Assistants
from an *ex officio* seat, they were still eligible to judgeships in
this tribunal, since the offices were not declared incompatible.
The final step in the separation of these two offices was not
taken until 1780, when the doctrine of a separation of the
functions of government was in the ascendency in the newly
created states of the Union. It was then enacted by the
Assembly that, " Whereas it is incompatible with the constitution of this state, for the legislative or judicial and powers of
government to be vested in the same persons," " for the future,
no member, either of the upper or lower house of Assembly
. . . . shall exercise the office of a justice of the superior court,
within this state, from and after the next election."[5] This
principle, once asserted, rapidly gained ground, and in May,
1783, an act was passed excluding all judges of the Court of
Common Pleas from the General Assembly.[6] There was not,
however, an absolute separation of the judicial and legislative
functions until a much later date, since the Senate still exercised appellate jurisdiction in probate matter[7]—a power which

---

[1] Douglass' *Summary*, II, 96–7.
[2] Durfee's *Gleanings from the Judicial Hist. of R. I.*, 16–20.
[3] Any three of whom were sufficient to constitute a quorum. (*R. I. Col.
Rec.*, V, 226).
[4] Acts and Laws of R. I. from 1745 to 1750, ed. 1752, 27–8. Two sessions
of this court were to be held annually in each county of the colony.
[5] *R. I. Col. Rec.*, IX, 32.   [6] *Ibid.*, 690.
[7] Douglass' *Summary*, II, 85, 97.

it had inherited from the Colonial Council.[1]   In the early part
of the present century, this final remnant of judicial power was
transferred from the Senate to the Supreme Judicial Court,[2]
and the Senate as a body ceased to exercise *ex officio* judicial
authority.[3]

---

[1] In 1663 original probate jurisdiction was granted to the town councils
from whom appeals could be taken to the Governor and Council as "supreme
ordinary or judge of probates."

[2] Arnold (II, 157) says this change occurred in 1802, while Durfee (33)
says it occurred in 1822.

[3] The General Assembly, however, not only exercised judicial authority
throughout the colonial period, but after the beginning of statehood, it continued to do so in violation of the wholesome principle which had been
enacted in 1780 (see *supra*).   Under their oaths of office as legislators, the
members of the General Assembly assumed the responsibility of judges, and
it is difficult at times to decide from the colonial records whether the legislative or the judicial element predominated in its proceedings.   In fact, the
prudent limitations placed upon the range of its jurisdiction as prescribed
by one Assembly were often totally disregarded by another.   (Cf. Arnold,
I, 448, with *Ibid.*, 459-60).   Since it was above the courts it could exercise
unlimited authority, and therefore often came in conflict with them.   The
case of Mawney *vs.* Peirce came up before the Superior Court in 1752, and
was decided in favor of the plaintiff.   The defendant then appealed to the
Assembly as a *court* with appellate jurisdiction.   A new trial was granted
before the Assembly, and a verdict was rendered which "over-ruled the
decision of the highest actual judicial authority in the colony."   (*R. I.
Col. Rec.*, V, 359; Foster's *Town Government in R. I.*, J. H. Studies,
Fourth Series, II, 28).   The case of Randall *vs.* Robinson, as Judge Durfee
observes, not only "shows how utterly powerless the judiciary was under
the charter in any conflict with the legislature," but also "illustrates the
danger attending the exercise of judicial power by the legislative branch
of the government."   (*Gleanings, etc.*, 42).   In the celebrated case of
Trevett *vs.* Weeden, in 1786, the Assembly compelled the judges of the
Superior Court to answer for having declared one of its legislative acts un-
constitutional.   (*R. I. Col. Rec.*, X, 219-20; *Gleanings, etc.*, 52, *et seq*).
The decision of Chief Justice Ames in the case of Taylor *vs.* Place rendered in 1856 put an end to the exercise of judicial power by the Assembly.
That body delayed action in the case of Ives *vs.* Hazard which came up
shortly after the above decision was rendered, and was constantly before it
until February, 1860, when it was finally withdrawn.   Judge Durfee says
that "since then the Assembly has never, intentionally at least, encroached
upon the proper province of the judiciary."   (*Ibid.*, 65.)

Section IV.—*The Legislative Function.*

As has been noted, the Assistants were given legislative power by the second charter for the first time in Rhode Island history.[1] This charter declared the Governor or Deputy Governor and at least six Assistants necessary to constitute a quorum of the Assembly,—no reference being made to the Deputies as an essential part of that body.

Being thus constituted, the Assembly was given power to admit freemen,[2] to establish courts and other necessary offices, to elect and commission officers, to make and repeal laws and ordinances, to regulate elections, and to alter or annul sentences of the various courts of the colony.[3] The only restriction upon the exercise of this authority was imposed by an ingeniously worded clause of the charter which virtually annulled itself.[4] Not only was the legislature of the colony thus freed from royal interference, but it was also independent of the Governor, since he was not given the veto power.[5] The people of Rhode Island were therefore able to conduct their government in the same spirit of independence that had previously characterized the towns.

To be sure the failure of the charter to recognize the presence of a majority of the Deputies as necessary to constitute a quorum, was soon noted by the people, and in November, 1672,

---

[1] See *supra*, p. 58.

[2] This provision led to the final displacement of the charter in 1842.

[3] *R. I. Col. Rec.*, II, 9-10; Douglass' *Summary*, II, 81-2; Chalmers' *Annals*, 275.

[4] It required that the "laws, ordinances and constitutions soe made, bee not contrary and repugnant unto, butt, as neare as may bee, agreeable to the lawes of England, considering the nature and constitution of the place and people."

[5] In 1732 the law officers of the Crown decided that "by the charter of Rhode Island the governor had not veto power," and "more than all the King himself had no power reserved in the charter either to sanction or to veto any act of the Assembly that was not inconsistent with the laws of England." (Arnold, II, 108; Palfrey, IV, 130-1.)

the Deputies made a formal demand for greater recognition. After citing the privileges accorded all English citizens by the Petition of Rights, they claimed, as "representatives of the freemen" of the colony, the prerogatives accorded the House of Commons in England. A reform bill was then passed requiring: (1) That "noe tax nor rate from henceforth shall be made layde or levied on the inhabitants of this Collony, without the consent of the Deputys present pertaining to the whole Collony;"[1] and (2) That "in all weighty matters, wherein the King's honor is most concerned, and the peoples antient right and libertys most jeoparded . . . the Assembly shall be the major part of the Deputys belonging to the whole Collony, as there must be the major part of the Assistants (by the charter). Butt otherwise, such said act (if made without the major part of Deputys present), such said act shall be voyd and of none effect."[2] Thus, instead of equalizing the power of these bodies, an advantage was given to the Deputies, since they outnumbered the Assistants, and all acts were passed by a joint vote. This inequality was not offset until 1696,[3] when the Assembly was divided into two co-ordinate branches, each having power to originate any bill[4] and to negative the legis-

---

[1] In May, 1678, another restraint upon the taxing power of the Assembly was imposed by an act which required notice of all levies to be given in advance to all towns of the colony. (Arnold, I, 441).

[2] *R. I. Col. Rec.*, II, 472-3; Arnold, I, 364-5.

[3] For more than thirty years after its organization the Assembly was a unicameral body. This was not, however, in harmony with the ideas of the people, since the colonial records (II, 63) show that it had become "a long agitation" as early as the second meeting of the Assembly in October, 1664. By numerous expedients and compromises final action on the matter was deferred until May, 1696, when the two houses separated, and the Governor, Deputy Governor and ten Assistants became the Upper and the Deputies the Lower House of the Assembly. See Prof. T. F. Moran's *Rise and Development of the Bicameral System in America*, J. H. U. Studies, Thirteenth Series, V, 22-6.

[4] In Rhode Island alone of all the New England colonies the Senate had undisputed power to originate money bills as late as the Revolution.

5

lative acts of the other.[1] The relations between the two bodies continued unaltered throughout the remainder of the colonial period, and in fact down to the present time.[2] When the colony became independent of Great Britain the charter as a constitution of civil government was abrogated, yet the form of government which was established by it was continued by common consent without any essential change,[3] and throughout the constitution-making period which followed the close of the struggle with England, Rhode Island, like Connecticut, retained her old charter as a state constitution. After the close of the Revolutionary War, the Upper House of the Assembly, which had been called the "Council," was dignified by the more republican and euphonious title of "Senate."

Section V.—The Constitution of 1842.

This instrument provided that the government of the state should still be "distributed into three departments, the legislative, executive, and judicial."[4]

The chief executive power was vested in a Governor and a Lieutenant Governor, both of whom were elected annually.[5]

The judicial power was vested in a Supreme Court and in such inferior courts as the General Assembly might ordain and establish.[6]

The legislative function was vested in a General Assembly which continued to exercise the powers it had "hitherto exercised, unless prohibited by the constitution."[7] It was com-

---

[1] Rhode Island is the only New England State in which the Governor and Deputy Governor are still *ex officio* members of the Senate and the Governor is denied a veto power.

[2] See *infra.*

[3] Pease and Niles' *Gazetteer of Conn. and R. I.* (1819), 313.   [4] Art. III.

[5] Art. VII, Sec. 1. In 1854 the pardoning power was placed in the hands of the Governor "with the advice and consent of the Senate." (Amendments to the Constitution of 1842, Art. II.)

[6] Art. X, Sec. 1.   [7] Art. IV, Sec. 10.

posed of two branches—a House of Representatives and a
Senate.[1] The former was based upon population, each town
being entitled to at least one Representative and not more than
one-sixth of the whole number.[2] The Upper House was based
upon a different and somewhat arbitrary principle,—only one
Senator being elected annually from each town regardless of
population.[3] As in colonial times, both bodies continued to
meet together in "Grand Committee" for the transaction of
matters pertaining to elections.[4] When sitting apart, the
powers and privileges of both continued to be co-equal in
every respect. The now effete and totally illogical principle
of limiting the prerogative of the Senate in the origination
of money-bills was still ignored as it had always been in Rhode
Island. Due caution was shown in regard to public finance
by the incorporation of a provision that a two-thirds vote " of
the members elected to each house," was necessary to appro-
priate "public money or public property for local or private
purposes."[5] The spirit of regard for the primary source of
authority which has always characterized Rhode Island both
as a colony and a state was not totally ignored in this constitution. There were two provisions which restricted the power of
the General Assembly : (1) It was not allowed, except under
certain circumstances, " to incur State debts to an amount ex-

---

[1]Art. IV, Sec. 2.   [2]Art. V, Sec. 1.
[3]Art. VI, Sec. 1. This protection of the rights of the minority is one of
the fundamental principles for which Rhode Island contended upon the
formation of the Federal Constitution. This "most conservative element
in their whole system of government" was incorporated into the Constitution of 1842 in order to "maintain unimpaired the equal rights of every
section of the State," and to "prevent any one interest from engrossing a
dangerous portion of political power" (Mr. Goddard's *Address on the Occasion of the change in the Civil Government of R. I.,* 31), since such a city as
Providence, which at that time had 25,000 inhabitants and therefore wielded
in the House one-sixth of the power, was entitled to exert no more power
in the Senate than the town of Jamestown, which at that time had less than
400 inhabitants. (*Ibid.,* 30.)
[4]Art. IV, Sec. 18; VIII, Secs. 3, 7 ; X, Secs. 4, 5.   [5]Art. IV, Sec. 14.

ceeding fifty thousand dollars," " without the express consent
of the people ; "[1] and (2) all bills for the creation of corporations, with certain stipulated exceptions, should " be continued
until another election of members of the General Assembly,"
and " such public notice of the pendency thereof" should " be
given as may be required by law."[2]

No changes were made in the personnel of the Senate. The
Governor still held his position as *ex officio* President of that
body, and as such, had a casting vote " in case of equal division," but no veto power.[3] The Lieutenant Governor also
retained his position as an *ex officio* member, having equal
privileges with the rest of the Senators.[4]

As in other states, the Senate retained a fragment of judicial
authority in its power to try impeachments.[5] A person convicted in such a trial was also liable to criminal " indictment,
trial, and punishment according to law."[6]

---

[1] Art. IV, Sec. 13.   [2] Art. IV, Sec. 17.   [3] Art. VI, Sec. 2.
[4] Art. VI, Sec. 1.   [5] Art. XI, Sec. 2.   [6] Art. XI, Sec. 3.

CHAPTER V.

CONCLUSIONS.

Section I.—*Origin of the New England Senates.*

If the facts here set forth have been correctly apprehended, the State Senates of New England did not originate in a desire to transplant to American soil the English House of Lords; but on the contrary, they are in their most important and essential features, the results of a natural course of development under circumstances and conditions peculiar to the colonies themselves.[1] To be sure they bear some crude analogies to the House of Lords, but analogies alone are dangerous premises from which to deduce conclusions as to the origin of institutions, since they may be due not to imitation but to common race instincts or to similarity of circumstances.[2]

---

[1] This phase of the subject has been presented by James Harvey Robinson in the *Annals of Amer. Acad.*, I, 203–243, and by William C. Morey in *ibid.*, 529–557, also in *ibid.*, IV, pt. 1, 201–232.

[2] "A strong current of similar events will produce coincidences in the history of nations whose whole institutions are distinct; much more will like circumstances force similarly constituted nations into like expedients; nay, great legislators will think together even if the events that suggest the thought be of the most dissimilar character. No amount of analogy between two systems can by itself prove the actual derivation of the one from the other." (Stubbs' *Constitutional Hist. of Eng.*, second edition, I, 207).

"We see the same political phænomena repeating themselves over and over again in various times and places, not because of any borrowing or imitation, conscious or unconscious, but because the like circumstances have led to the like results." (Freeman's *Comparative Politics*, 32).

These analogies between the Senate and the House of Lords lose their force as arguments when we consider the facts that:

1. The Councils from which the Senates developed, originated in ideas foreign to the English political system. The charters upon which the government of the colonies were based, owe their origin not to the political but the commercial policy of the mother country.[1] Hence the Council of Massachusetts was evolved from the Board of Directors of a trading company[2] and furnished in turn, the model for those of Connecticut[3] and New Hampshire;[4] while in Rhode Island it was merely a revival of the Hebrew Court of Elders,[5] and previous to the granting of the charter of 1663 by which its government was assimilated to the common model, this body had no legislative power whatever.

2. The transition from Council to Senate was not made through any conscious efforts to conform to British models. The preceding pages of this study have shown that the successive stages of this development,—the introduction of the representative system,[6] the granting of a negative power,[7] the introduction of the bicameral system,[8] the loss of *ex officio* membership in the Councils,[9] the gradual diminution and final disappearance of their executive and judicial authority, and the differentiation of the powers and privileges of the two branches of the legislatures[10]—either followed from intercolonial influences or from efforts on the part of the colonists to remove the points of friction in their crudely organized governments, and thus to adapt their primitive institutions to American conditions. If, again, the colonists had imitated a common model in the development of this institution their

---

[1] For an able presentation of this subject see Prof. Morey's *Genesis of a Written Constitution*, Annals of the Amer. Acad., Vol. I, p. 529 *et seq.*, April, 1891.

[2] *Supra*, p. 10.   [3] *Supra*, pp. 28, 30, note 2.

[4] *Supra*, p. 46.   [5] *Supra*, p. 56.   [6] *Supra*, pp. 18, 56, note 1.

[7] *Supra*, pp. 20, 36–7, 46, 65.   [8] *Supra*, pp. 20–1, 37, 46, 65.

[9] *Supra*, pp. 21–2.   [10] *Supra*, pp. 15, note 1, 22–3, 37.

results would have exhibited more features in common. On the contrary, however, at the formation of the Federal Constitution they differed in almost every characteristic feature,— in size,[1] composition,[2] qualification,[3] basis of election,[4] powers and privileges.[5] In fact, as Prof. Morey forcibly observes, "it might well be said that they were common only in that feature, in which they differed from the English House of Lords, namely, the fact that they were all based upon popular election."[6]

---

[1] The size of the early state Senates in New England were as follows: Massachusetts, thirty-one (*supra*, p. 27, note 2); Connecticut, twelve (*supra*, pp. 30, note 4, 38); New Hampshire, twelve (*supra*, p. 52), and Rhode Island, ten (*supra*, p. 58).

[2] In Massachusetts the Governor and Lieutenant-Governor ceased to be *ex officio* members of the Senate in the colonial era (*supra*, pp. 21-2). In Connecticut both retained their seats in this body until 1818 (*supra*, pp. 38–9). In New Hampshire the Senate was composed of twelve Senators, presided over by the President of the state who had a vote equal with the others (*supra*, p. 52). In Rhode Island the Governor and the Lieutenant-Governor still have a seat in the Senate the former being *ex officio* President (*supra*, pp. 66, note 1, 68).

[3] The qualifications for Senator after the Revolution were as follows: Massachusetts—must be an inhabitant of the state five years and of the district at the time of election, have a freehold estate of £300 or a personal estate of £600 (*supra*, p. 26, note 1); Connecticut—must be a citizen of the state (*supra*, p. 39, note 2); New Hampshire—must be a protestant, possessed of a freehold estate of £200 within the state, an inhabitant of the state for seven years preceding election and of the district from which chosen at the time of election (*supra*, p. 23); Rhode Island—citizenship in one of the four principal towns of the colony (*supra*, p. 67).

[4] In Massachusetts the Senators were chosen from electoral districts (*supra*, p. 27, note 2); in Connecticut from the state at large (*supra*, p. 38); in New Hampshire from electoral districts (*supra*, p. 52); and in Rhode Island from the different towns of the state (*supra*, p. 67).

[5] In Massachusetts (*supra*, p. 27), and New Hampshire (*supra*, p. 53) the Lower House alone could originate money bills, while in Rhode Island it could be done by either branch (*supra*, p. 65, note 4). In Massachusetts and New Hampshire the Upper House alone had power to try impeachments.

[6] Annals Amer. Acad., IV, pt. I, p. 22, September, 1893.

Section II.—Forces which gave Direction to the Development.[1]

It is difficult to account in a satisfactory way for all the phenomena which appear in the history of this evolution from Council to Senate. Of the many complicated causes which determined the course of this development, from time to time, the following appear to the writer as worthy of mention :

1. *Limitation of the Number of Counsellors.*—In all these colonies the number of Counsellors was fixed by charter and could not therefore increase with the growth of population[2] as could the Deputies or Representatives chosen by the towns. Since the General Courts were at first unicameral bodies, this limitation threatened to destroy the power of the Councils which formed a hopelessly small and constantly diminishing proportion in the membership of these bodies. This cause, enforced by the constant clashing of authority, led to two important results in the evolution of the Councils : (1) The granting of a negative vote to each of the constituent parts of the General Courts over the acts of the other,[3] and (2) The introduction of the bicameral system.[4]

2. *Extent of Authority, and Growth of the Colonies.*—The Councils not only enjoyed a legislative power which was coordinate with that of the popular branches, but their authority also extended originally over the executive and judicial domains. Thus the body which was incapable of increase was granted powers which extended into every department of government, while the larger and more elastic body, numerically speaking, was preëminently a legislative body. Upon the

---

[1] No author, within the knowledge of the writer, has hitherto attempted to go into the details of this discussion.

[2] It is not probable that the colonists, who were jealous of the aristocratic tendencies of these bodies, desired to increase their number. See *supra.*

[3] *Supra*, pp. 20, 36–7. New Hampshire was an exception. Having had the benefit of the experiences of Massachusetts she settled this question without a struggle (*supra*, p. 46).

[4] *Supra*, pp. 20–1, 37, 65.

growth of the colonies and the consequent increase of public business, it became impossible for the Counsellors to attend to their numerous and constantly accumulating duties. Since their number was not permitted to increase to a degree commensurate with the burdens of their office, the problem could only be solved by restricting the scope of their authority. This resulted in a diminution of their executive and judicial duties in the following ways : (1) By the delegation of their powers, especially those of a judicial nature ;[1] (2) By the creation of judges outside their ranks ;[2] and (3) By a reduction of the number of Counsellors necessary to constitute a quorum.[3]

3. *Illogical Principle upon which Power was Distributed.*— Instead of having a wholesome system of checks and balances, the colonial governments present a union of the most incompatible principles of authority. The Counsellors were at the same time intrusted with the making, the interpreting, and the executing of laws. As members of the General Courts, which constituted the supreme judicial tribunal of the colonies, they heard and were allowed either to help determine or at least to express opinions on cases of appeal from their verdicts as courts of the first instance. They were also required to act upon bills for the regulation of the judicial system—in which they were of course personally concerned—before such bills could have the force of law. The most serious defect of such a distribution of power was perhaps its effect upon the offices of relatively small importance. Since the Counsellors acted in several capacities, they were usually chosen with regard to their most important function. This principle of choice might lead to the selection of an efficient legislative body, but since those most efficient in legislation are not always the most capable in administration and adjudication, one or both of these functions must suffer by such a union. The colonists saw and opposed some of these incongruities

---

[1]*Supra*, pp. 17, 33–5, 45, 62.   [2]*Ibid.*   [3]*Supra*, p. 10, note 2.

from time to time, but were unable to effect the necessary changes before the formation of their State Constitutions.

4. *Introduction of the Idea of a Complete Separation of the Functions of Government.*—Although the growth of the colonies and the illogical distribution of power tended to a differentiation of governmental functions, it is not probable that this principle would have been so clearly and uniformly applied as it is at present, if the Montesquieu[1] doctrine of a complete separation of the functions of government had not gained an ascendency in the colonies just as they were entering the great constitution-making epoch in their history. Hence the introduction of this idea must have hastened, at least, the final step in the evolution of the Senate.

5. *Inter-Colonial Influences.*—This force is particularly noticeable in the New England colonies, since their laws and institutions are alike in many respects, and come for the most part from the same mother colony. This natural predilection was further increased by their close proximity to each other and their isolation from the mother country, their homogeneity in race and language, and their common dangers and ambitions. These things produced an intercourse among them, which resulted in the general dissemination of American principles.

6. *English Charters and Precedents.*—The various charters of the New England colonies have a common origin and therefore resemble in many respects. They furnished the broad

---

[1] "Zuerst hat Montesquieu das moderne Princip mit Nachdruck und mit Erfolg verkündet." (Bluntschli's *Statslehre*, 588.)

"Lorsque, dans, la même personne ou dans le même corps de magistrature, la puissance législative est réunie à la puissance exécutrice, il n'y a point de liberté, parce qu'on peut craindre que le même monarque ou le même sénat ne fasse des lois tyranniques pour les exécuter tyranniquement.

"Il n'y a point encore de liberté si la puissance de juger n'est pas séparée de la puissance législative et de l'exécutrice. Si elle etait jointe à la puissance législative, le pouvoir sur la vie et la liberté des citoyens serait arbitraire; car le juge serait législateur. Si elle était jointe à la puissance exécutrice, le juge pourrait avoir la force d'un oppresseur." (Montesquieu's *De L'Esprit de Lois*, Book XI, Ch. VI.)

outlines of government and thus gave general direction to the development of institutions which are distinctly American. The colonists were also conversant with the English Constitution and began at an early day to cite such English precedents as might be in their favor. The extent of both these influences may, however, be easily exaggerated, since the most beneficent features of colonial government,—the representative system for example[1]—were not established by any charters until they had become established in the colonies; and again, the assertion of a claim to the benefits bestowed by any particular English precedent was by no means tantamount to a concession on the part of those with whose ideas or interests it came in conflict. For instance, the right of the popular branch to originate money bills was asserted in Massachusetts at a comparatively early date. This demand was doubtless based upon English precedent, but since the charter contained no such provision, the point at issue was not finally conceded without a series of conflicts extending over a long period of time. In fact, English precedents had to fight their battles anew on American soil, and were seldom incorporated into the government of the colonies before they had shown themselves worthy of a place in our political system. Hence those features which were usually claimed as an inheritance and consciously adopted, were " not so much the customary forms which entered into the structure of the British government as those chartered privileges which might serve to protect them from the supervision and interference of autocratic power."[2]

Section III.—Inherited Characteristics of the Senates.

Although, as has been noted, the Councils in the New England colonies presented many essential points of contrast to each other, there is, nevertheless, a certain degree of unity

---

[1]*Supra*, p. 18.

[2] Morey's *First State Constitutions*, Annals Amer. Acad., Vol. IV, pt. 1, 32, September, 1893.

in this diversity. ˙They exhibited certain features in common which have been transmitted, to their successors. The most striking of these are the contrasts between the Councils and the Lower Houses of the Assemblies on the following points :

1. *Size.*—The Councils were always the smaller of the two branches of the Legislature. Their number was usually fixed by charter and was not, therefore, subject to the degree of variation that is noticeable in the Lower Houses.

2. *Personnel.*—The Councils were composed of the more dignified and conservative portions of the population. The Representatives were chosen from among the people and were therefore more closely in touch with them, and hence more radical in principle.

3. *Basis of Selection.*[1]—The Counsellors represented a larger constituency than the Representatives, who were always chosen by towns or hundreds.

4. *Term of Office.*—The Counsellors were chosen for a long term,[2] while the Representatives were always chosen for a brief period.

---

[1] The method by which the Counsellors were chosen varied from time to time. See *supra.*

[2] In Massachusetts and Connecticut the Counsellors had at first practically a life-tenure. See *supra.*